Attitude + Advocacy

+ Adaptive Technology

= Academic Success

Attitude + Advocacy + Adaptive Technology = Academic Success

14 Proven Strategies for Students with Learning Challenges, Their Parents and Educators

Plus a Guide for Getting into the Right Post-Secondary Program

K-12 and Post-Secondary

Learning Disabilities, Asperger's Syndrome, ADHD, Autism, Head Injuries or Aphasia

Natalie Phelps Tate, M.S. Ed.

Individual Learning Solutions Inc.

www.individuallearningsolutions.org

Published by Individual Learning Solutions Inc.

www.individuallearningsolutions.org

Printed in the United States of America

Tate, Natalie Phelps.

Attitude + Advocacy + Adaptive Technology = Academic Success
14 Proven Strategies for Students with Learning Challenges, Their Parents and Educators Plus a Guide for Getting into the Right Post-Secondary Program

ISBN-10: 1508972400

ISBN-13: 978-1508972402

1. Learning Differences   2. Learning Disabilities   3. ADHD
4. Autism   5. Asperger's Syndrome   6. Head Injuries
7. Aphasia   8. Social Skills   9. Post-Secondary Programs

Book Cover Design By John Tate

Contents

III.   ADAPTIVE TECHNOLOGIES

Acknowledgements

I owe my deepest gratitude to my mother and father for their belief in me and for always raising the bar. I would like to thank my educators, teachers and tutors who helped me through the years and who kept an open mind toward the accommodations I have needed. I want to thank St. Louis Books on Tape, Learning Ally (formerly RFB&D), and my college and university support services for creating and providing my books on tape. Special thanks to Dr. William S. Coxe, Jean Moog, Victoria Kozak Robinson, Paula Folwell, Paul Kosuth, Sandy Rafferty, Louise Shapleigh, Damaris Miltenberger, Dr. Richard Collins, Mary Gravel, Steve Gilpatrick, and especially Katherine Fogarty. You have all helped me in priceless ways throughout my journey. I couldn't have done any of it without you.

Endorsements

John C. Cary
Superintendent of Schools

Natalie Phelps Tate's Attitude +Advocacy + Adaptive Technology = Academic Success is an easy read, but packed with great strategies for students with learning challenges to maneuver successfully through school and college. But that's not all. This book also gives great tips to parents and teachers on providing a supportive environment for these students as well. It's a "must-read" for students with learning issues who want to beat the odds and obtain academic success, just as the author has done herself, and the adults who support them.

John C. Cary
Superintendent of Schools
Special School District of St. Louis County, Missouri
12110 Clayton Road / Town & Country, MO 63131
Located in St. Louis County, Missouri, SSD is a nationwide leader in providing special education services and technical education.

Jean Sachar Moog
Moog Center for Deaf Education

Practical, informative, honest, candid, no-nonsense approach, upbeat, inspirational – these are words that describe the content and writing style of Natalie Phelps Tate in this collection of strategies and tips for students with learning challenges and their parents, educators, and friends. Tate speaks from first-hand experience as an individual with learning challenges. Her own achievements demonstrate the power of her strategies and the possibilities for success.

Jean Sachar Moog
Moog Center for Deaf Education
A Certified Moog Program
12300 South Forty Drive
St. Louis, MO 63141

Sandra K. Gilligan, Director
Churchill Center & School

*Your own personal story is poignant yet uplifting as you describe your transformation from a six-year-old child suffering a brain aneurysm to a very successful adult with a Masters' degree.
*Your emphasis on the need for students to have a positive attitude and to believe in themselves.

*The inclusion of specific, practical ideas, along with examples, that students can implement to be self-advocates through high school and college.
*This is a comprehensive manual that can be used by students, teachers, and parents…chock-full of practical ideas.
*I really like your simple, straightforward style of writing.

Sandra K. Gilligan, Director
Churchill Center & School
1021 Municipal Center Drive
St Louis, MO 63131

Rosalyn S. Lowenhaupt Educational Consultant Independent School Placement Service of St. Louis, LLC

Natalie Phelps Tate has woven her experience as a childhood stroke survivor and her academic knowledge of psychology to create a practical book which will help students with learning disabilities make the most of their education. With model letters to teachers and lists of technological aids, Ms. Tate presents a useful guide for motivated LD students and their families.

Rosalyn S. Lowenhaupt Educational Consultant
801 S. Skinker Blvd. #15C
St. Louis, MO 63105

Kathryn Burrow Fogarty M.S.
M.S. in Special Education
Educational Consultant

In this book Natalie Phelps Tate presents her own personal story that should inspire any student experiencing learning challenges to face and triumph over their difficulties, allowing them to achieve success in school. But she not only offers inspiration and motivation, she also provides a practical guide. As a person who managed her own learning challenges exceptionally well and as a degreed educator, Natalie brings together these two perspectives to offer a cornucopia of valuable information for students, parents and educators so all will benefit from this incomparable text.

Victoria Kozak Robinson, M.A. Ed.
B.S. in Speech & Hearing
M.A. Ed. in Education
Former Headmistress, Central Institute for the Deaf

Natalie Phelps Tate didn't start out her life with a learning disability. As a young, bright, elementary school student, she had a major stroke which led to her significant learning disability. She completely lost the ability to understand and to use spoken language. Natalie had to re-learn how to walk, read, write, count, add, subtract, understand language and talk. She approached her challenges with a very supportive family, a very positive attitude and with a complete team effort toward rehabilitation. From the first day I met with her, she was determined, optimistic, hard-working and delightful. No task was too daunting for her. She was ready to do whatever was needed to regain her skills. Her sense of humor and her spirit were well intact! While others assisted Natalie with regaining physical mobility, I had the golden opportunity to help her regain the wonderful gift of language. She used her intellect, her determination and her sense of humor to help her wander through the fray, back to the confident, happy, smart, well-adjusted girl she had been before. Now that Natalie is a successful young wife, mother and teacher, she has found yet another way to give back. You, the reader, have the golden opportunity to learn from Natalie about how to give or to receive help as individuals, families or service providers. Determination, effort, team work and support will drive your success! Don't forget your positive attitude, which is key!

Suzanne Lanning-Ventura, Ph.D.
Former teacher/advisor, Brehm Preparatory School

Natalie Phelps Tate, M.S. Ed. is a courageous author. Her enthusiasm and fire are observed when reading her book. She has shared with her readers the navigation basics for students, parents and educators. The information is clear and precise with plans practical and useful. The book is a wide-ranging exploration of the countless ways in which information is learned and sustained. Brimming with information and wit, Natalie is most of all interested in what will benefit so many.

Personal History

I think it might give you added perspective if I begin by telling you a little of my history as a student, and later as an educator, with Learning Disabilities. When I was six years old, out of the blue, I had a cerebral aneurysm which left me without any expressive speech, right-side paralysis, two visual field cuts and acute aphasia[1].

After my recovery from surgery, the hospital recommended indefinite institutionalization in a rehabilitation center. My prognosis for a normal life was grim. My parents weren't willing to give up without a fight and believed that my home environment could stimulate memory and recovery. They brought me home.

---

[1] Aphasia is the loss or impairment of the ability to use speech due to a brain injury.

My parents took me to Central Institute for the Deaf in St. Louis for intellectual diagnostic testing because CID was adept at evaluating non-verbal children. Part way through the testing, CID's director, Jean Moog, came into the cubicle to observe. That afternoon she offered to adapt a World War One head-injury therapy to my needs and offered me a place in their kindergarten. It was a miracle. I spent several years at CID regaining my speech.

The worst of my paralysis responded to extensive physical therapy, but there had been irreversible damage to the language sections of my brain. In spite of intense work in a variety of remedial reading programs, I was not able to learn to read anywhere close to my grade level and some of the aphasia remains. I had "acquired" a severe learning disability.

I went on to attend Churchill Center & School (formerly Churchill School), an excellent remedial program for students with learning disabilities, also in St. Louis, Missouri.

My testing in middle school indicated that I would be lucky to graduate with a basic Certificate of Completion and that my parents had better investigate vocational training. Any notion of college was a joke.

Somewhere along the line I had decided that I wanted to be a psychologist and that required college, and a good one, as a first step to graduate school. By eighth grade, which I attended at Brehm Preparatory School, for students with learning disabilities, in Carbondale, Illinois, I had begun to develop strategies to make this goal attainable. Brehm taught me all kinds of strategies: compensation strategies, advocacy strategies, adaptive technological strategies, interpersonal strategies, whatever it took to learn the way my damaged brain needed to learn. And many of these strategies ultimately worked.

In sophomore year I decided to take a risk and leave the supportive environment of "special" schools in order to build a resume for college and I enrolled in my local high school, Horton Watkins in Ladue, Missouri. The decision proved a good one. The support and teachers were amazing and I flourished - of course with hard work.

Only a year behind my chronological class, I graduated from my local high school as a member of The National Honor Society with a 3.75 GPA, and was accepted early admissions by my first choice college, Bates College in Maine. Bates ranked as one of the top 20 liberal arts colleges in the country. I made Dean's List my freshman year and graduated in four years. Bates had a short-term semester in April and May. While many fellow students "played" during their free short-terms, I interned at my former boarding school for students with learning disabilities. That led to my choice of graduate programs.

Through my four years at Bates I had fallen in love with the state of Maine and I desperately needed a break from academics and a chance to recharge my batteries. I loved the weather and I adored the cold and beautiful white snow. I found a refurbished 1740s ferry inn on the Kennebec River and spent a magical year with my horses, dog and cat.

The following spring, I applied to grad school at Southern Illinois University, Carbondale in the Educational Psychology Department and was accepted. I started grad school January of 2002. In the summer of 2006, I completed my Master's in Educational Psychology, with an emphasis in learning disabilities, at the University of Illinois at Carbondale. I also worked at Brehm Preparatory School as a Transition Specialist Intern, evaluating the academic, social and emotional potential of our graduating students and coaching the students and their parents how to make the most appropriate post-secondary choice: vocational, two-year, or four-year college. After earning my degree, I taught psychology and career development classes at John A. Logan College in Carterville, IL.

I am presently director of Individual Learning Solutions Inc., (www.individuallearningsolutions.org or www.ilsinc.org) a not-for-profit organization dedicated to providing services to and "coaching" students with learning challenges and their families. Our mission is to empower students with a wide spectrum of learning challenges to reach their full academic, social, and emotional potential by offering and coordinating of a variety of services. Our services include coaching, counseling, tutoring, family counseling, support groups, speech and language therapy, reading programs, educating siblings and parents about the child's learning challenges, school selection, post-secondary and career advising, and equine therapy.

We promote family wellness by addressing the needs of the whole "special" family and coordinating disparate services. Individual Learning Solutions envisions its role as a personal advocate from initial diagnosis through career selection. ILS can provide or coordinate the multitude of services students require throughout their academic career. We share strategies and knowledge with the special needs community through research, publications, and presentations.

I married in 2011 and had my son, Harrison in 2012.

In many ways I have reached the goals I dreamed of so many years ago. It has been a long, but always rewarding journey. I believe that many of the strategies I developed along the way might be worth the time and might change the lives of students. I believe that these strategies can be adapted to students' individual needs and empower them to achieve their goals.

Introduction

Welcome. My name is Natalie P. Tate. The title of this book is *Attitude, Advocacy, Adaptive Technologies = Academic Success: 14 Proven Strategies for Students with Learning and Social Challenges and Their Parents and Educators.* My goal in writing this is to provide encouragement and strategies that can make a dramatic difference in the academic lives of students with learning challenges. These are 14 primary strategies that I have developed and used myself over the past 30+ years in coping with my learning disability, both as a student and as an educator. These strategies have enabled me to reach my goals. I believe that these 14 strategies can be used by most students with a broad range of learning and social challenges to achieve success.

Diagnosis definitions and legal classifications for students with challenges change over time. Whatever the labels are today, each student is "one of a kind" and has unique strengths to build upon. These proven strategies showcase those strengths and I believe that they can empower students with learning challenges to achieve their goals.

For your convenience, all sample letters, information lists and questionnaires are available for you to download and personalize from my website: www.ilsinc.org.

Each section in this book ends with a section of additional insights designed especially for students, parents and for educators just like the section below.

Especially for:

<u>Students</u>

Having learning challenges is not easy or fun. It means extra time and effort for many tasks and probably for your whole life. It means that you will have to learn to take responsibility earlier, you will need to learn to advocate for yourself and in general, you will have to grow up faster than your peers.

The good news is that you will find there are many people willing to teach and mentor you. There are many resources and strategies at your fingertips. There are many excellent post-secondary programs with support for your learning challenges from vocational programs to post-graduate degrees. Digital books, the Internet and adaptive technology put lifelong learning easily within your grasp.

Recognize that setbacks are learning opportunities, not failures. Take the time to savor and celebrate every victory. You will have earned it.

It is most important to dream your dreams, believe in your potential and know that miracles are possible—even if you have to make them happen yourself.

Parents

Always remember, no one knows your child as you do. Your role as advocate, coach and cheerleader for your child with learning differences is essential to his or her success. There is so much you can do to put their dreams within their reach. The amount of information and multiple options available to you will often seem overwhelming. I hope the suggestions and strategies in these pages make you aware of the multitude of resources available to you for getting the level of support your child needs and deserves. There are so many tools and people and support groups who are there to help if only you know where to look. If your child uses ten percent of the strategies from these pages, it can make a real difference. Guard against overprotection and complacency. Plan, always, for the next step. Seek all opportunities to raise the bar for your child. Above all, celebrate all successes and expect miracles!

Educators

These students require all your teaching insights. Their parents need all your advocacy and mentoring skills. These students do walk a tightrope between accomplishment and failure and you often have the power to affect their outcome. These students are often worth your best efforts. Try to save some energy and enthusiasm for their dreams

ATTITUDE

STRATEGY ONE
Believe in Possibilities

You might guess from my history that my first strategy is that students with learning challenges, and those who advise them, must believe in "possibilities." Success and achievement are about "possibilities," not about "limitations." It is a crucial matter of attitude.

At many stages of your journey you will face predictions that will seem to set limits on accomplishment. Diagnosis itself can seem to place students into limiting cubbyholes rather than to liberate them to pursue known solutions. Labels frighten, paralyze and taunt. Focus can easily shift from *can do* to *can't do*. It is crucial to recognize that any evaluation or judgment is an opinion subject to error and is a snapshot in time subject to change. I am not against acceptance and realism, but always leave room for hope.

I am warning against blindly accepting the experts' recommendations. The doctors, evaluators, administrators, teachers and all the others who pass judgments about a student are most likely very competent. The opinions they offer might be very professionally based, and I am sure they have the best interests of the student at heart. But always remember that they can be wrong. They can underestimate your student's potential. I am warning against accepting expert opinions and testing results as limitations carved in stone. It is not that I do not respect the experts; they are often right. It is not that I discount the value of standard assessments; they are great diagnostic tools and can highlight legitimate strengths and weaknesses for future focus. But the student with challenges, and his or her advisors, cannot allow either the experts or their assessments to become "limitations." The students and their advisors must learn to look beyond these indicators for each student's individual strengths and motivations that can empower them to mitigate often-dire predictions.

Standardized, diagnostic tests are extremely useful for getting "a handle" on a student's present level of performance, for understanding their learning strengths and weaknesses, for measuring trends in their acquisition of skills and for exposing areas of continuing weakness.

However, my experience is that most testing done by public agencies is designed to identify weaknesses and to qualify the student for special services. It is important not to be overly discouraged by the deficits these test results expose and to remember to focus on the student's strengths as well. You need to understand that when a student takes these tests, more often than not, the desired outcome is for the scores to reflect the student's deficits and their need for specialized services and accommodations. This is terrific when you are looking for services, but it can be counterproductive when you are applying to colleges or other programs. In these cases you want the testing to demonstrate "competencies" and "suggest" the possibility of success in specific programs.

Diagnostic testing usually results in a "label" for the student's disability: Attention Deficit Hyperactivity Disorder (ADHD), Learning Disability (LD), Autism Spectrum Disorders, and so on. These particular labels generally correspond to definitions in the DSM-5. The DSM-5 is the *Diagnostic and Statistical Manual of Mental Disorders* (DSM) published by the American Psychiatric Association. In addition to defining criteria for the classification of mental disorders, it defines personality disorders and intellectual disabilities as well as assessments of functioning for children. The definitions and "labels" are used by most private evaluators and insurance companies in determining what services they will offer or cover. Public school districts have similar classifications. If students' present characteristics of ADHD or Asperger's and these behaviors interfere with school participation in some way; the school might classify the student as "Other Health Impaired." Sometimes the classification of "Emotionally Disturbed" is used if the student has significant emotional/behavioral challenges that interfere with learning. "Learning Disability" is another educational label.

While some parents understandably resist labeling their children in this way, it is generally necessary in order to qualify for services within a school district or for insurance coverage. Neither parents nor educators should be held captive by these labels as indicators of potential achievement. They do not define the child, only some of his or her deficits.

The DSM and school classifications have changed over time. The most current revision of the medical manual is the fifth edition ("DSM-5"), 2013. Some educational classifications changed when the federal law guiding special education services was revised and renamed from PL94-142 to IDEA in 1990. Criteria for these classifications have also changed as new information about various learning challenges has developed.

As you can see, definitions can change substantially over time, sometimes a relatively short time. The definition of a "label" for a deficit learned by a teacher or lay person during their training several years ago and definition for the same "label" applied to your student today might have changed significantly. Prejudices and misinformation can easily attach to labels. It is important to always keep in mind that every child is "one of a kind" even when labeled according to the DSM-5 or IDEA, and it is important to remember that no labeling is static.

Students with learning challenges and those who advocate for them should not allow these labels to become barriers and must constantly encourage others to look beyond students' labels to their individual potential.

Parents, educators and evaluators need always keep in mind that the student with learning and or social challenges is much more than his or her paperwork. Miracles happen and possibilities are endless. Both the student and those who advise him or her need to believe this in their hearts. Almost as importantly, they need to devise strategies to convert others to this "attitude of possibilities" throughout the student's academic career.

On the drive home from the hospital the night of my surgery, my parents tell me that they found themselves on an icy highway behind a rusty old clunker that sported a bumper sticker that said, "Expect a Miracle." It was timely and profound advice for them that night and for all of us who deal with challenges.

ATTITUDE

Checklist for Strategy One:

- Believe in possibilities.

- Look beyond limitations.

- Use diagnosis and labels to qualify for services. Labels do not define the student.

- Believe in future miracles, but recognize today's realities.

Especially for:

Students

Do not let your diagnostic label limit your dreams. Try to nurture your courage to "dare" to be all that you can be. You have a unique brain. It is not like everyone else's. It "learns differently." There might be tasks that you cannot do or do well today. But you are young and your brain is "plastic," meaning that it grows and changes every day. There is no way for you or anyone else to know what your brain will be able to do tomorrow or next month or next year. You will never know if you do not "dare" to keep trying and experimenting. You will stumble often (safety nets are good things) but failures need not break you and you must have the courage to "dare" to have a chance of winning.

Parents

As parents, you are the student's foremost mentors and advocates. You are responsible for nurturing your children's belief in themselves, for encouraging their dreams and for maintaining their motivation. You are "the keeper of the flame" that is their hope of achieving their dreams. It will always be a tug-of-war between hope for the future and enough acceptance of the current reality to seek and find the services needed today. Truly, neither you nor anyone else knows what this child can achieve. It is your job to celebrate all successes and to keep all possibilities open. You must believe.

Educators

When reviewing a student's documentation at the beginning of the year, bear in mind that at best it represents only "a snapshot in time" of the student's skills and deficits. Do not let the student's diagnostic label define or limit your expectations. Your job in the limited time you have with that student is to change that snapshot for the better, hopefully a lot better. Your challenge is to find the unique key that unlocks the mind of that student to new concepts and new ways of learning. Many of your students can be reached by any competent teacher and they will thrive with routine instruction. This *individual* cannot. This student is largely dependent on your insight and imagination and your will to find the unique light that illuminates their path. It is a heavy burden, but also a great opportunity: With this student; you have the potential to truly change a life.

STRATEGY TWO

Value Teachers

Students with learning challenges must find strategies to convert their teachers to their "attitude of possibilities" and to recruit them as active supporters on their team.

Other students might thrive or at least survive with routine teaching, but in order to succeed in school, students with learning challenges need their teacher's very "best." They need teachers who will go the extra mile to discover and work with their unique learning style. They must motivate their teachers to stretch their creative teaching talents and to expend extra energy for them. The reality is that teachers are scarce resources with finite amounts of time and energy to devote to each student. Thus, students with learning challenges simply cannot afford to take their teachers for granted. They must find strategies to show their teachers that they are worthy of their teachers' best efforts, and motivate them to go that extra mile for them.

My experience has been that most teachers became teachers because they valued education and cared about positively influencing young lives. They worked hard to acquire their teaching skills and are dedicated to applying their skills effectively. Today teachers are too often overscheduled and under-respected. Both their students and their administrations often take them for granted. Many teachers feel that their opportunities to teach and mentor are being replaced by demands of discipline and paperwork.

I found that if I demonstrated a sincere desire to learn the material they were teaching and treated them with respect and consideration that my teachers would respond with amazing interest in my academic success. I think they were starved to do what they had come to teaching to do. I tried to show them that, with me, their skills could make a real difference. I tried to show them that I appreciated and respected their efforts with me. For the most part they responded.

While, of course, they had access to my academic special needs documentation and IEP information, I shared with them my needs for additional support (legal accommodations) and as well as I could in my own words, the reasons for them. We both understood that they were legally required to extend this extra help, but I tried to show my real appreciation for that extra work. I was unfailingly polite and friendly. A smile and wave in the halls in passing or a cheerful "Good morning, Mrs. X" can be very effective. Teachers are people who like to be liked and have their presence acknowledged just as you or I do.

In all my years of schooling, I have only had two teachers who were not supportive of me or my needed accommodations. One of the two, a high school chemistry teacher, did not "believe in" learning disabilities. I dropped the course. Later, when I was taking the course from another teacher, the first chemistry teacher (then retired) became my tutor. He was really enlightened by the experience! He came to see that, as my tutor, he gave me only the help I needed and that he did not "do" the work for me or "help" me take tests. He came to respect the extra time and effort I put into mastering the material, and he came to understand that accommodations for students with learning challenges are not unfair advantages or just an "easy out."

During my sophomore year in college, I experienced the other teacher who did not want to work with me. At the beginning of each school year or each semester, I gave my teachers a letter explaining my learning disability (we will discuss this in Strategy Eight) and allowed them the opportunity to ask questions if they wanted more information. My letter also explained how I used Internet resources and adaptive technology to research and write papers. When I handed in my first paper he accused me of plagiarism. His position was that if I could not read well I could not possibly find material in the library and could not write a coherent paper. Of course he had not read my accommodation letter and was completely unfamiliar with the Internet or adaptive technology screen readers and dictation. I finally had to have my other professors talk to him about my previous work with them. I'm not sure he ever really believed that the work was mine, but he didn't fail me. I didn't take any more courses from him either.

Considering how many courses I have taken through the years, those two teachers are a small minority compared to those who supported me. The successes I have had in school and beyond are due to the majority of teachers and professors who took the time to learn about my disability and worked with me to make my school experience a success. I will always be grateful to them and for their generosity with me.

From the other perspective, as a teacher in a community college, I have encountered students who, in my opinion, "use their diagnosis" as a crutch and as an excuse to avoid required assignments. After the first incident of such a situation, I call these students into my office to review their accommodation needs and to "coach" them on how to implement those accommodations responsibly. After second and third incidents, I have little sympathy for the student. On the other hand, I will spend many extra hours with any sincere student working on rewrites and reformatting tests or projects that in any way that allows the student to demonstrate mastery of the material. I am thrilled whenever I can give this type of student a "deserved" good grade. I feel that it is just as much an accolade for me as for them.

Some students' learning challenges include difficulties with attention, organization and impulsive behaviors. These students need to develop the skills to "explain" these offensive behaviors and to apologize appropriately for them. Social skills deficits are an important component of many learning challenges. The affected students and their teachers need to be able to communicate cooperatively and problem-solve successfully when these behaviors occur. Role playing and setting very specific behavioral goals can be effective strategies in promoting appropriate and respectful relationship building between student and teacher.

To be effective, all these strategies must be rooted in a student's sincere respect for good teachers, both as dedicated professionals and as valued human beings. This attitude of respect, of course, applies to counselors, tutors and anyone else who can contribute to the student's success. All these mentors must be motivated to believe in the "possibilities" of the student with learning challenges.

<u>Checklist for Strategy Two:</u>

- Don't take teachers for granted.
- Motivate counselors, tutors, and professionals to become mentors.
- With patience, the few teachers resistant to a student's needs can be converted to allies.
- Resist the temptation to use your diagnosis as a crutch.

Especially for:

Students

In some schools, it is "cool" for students (and sometimes for parents) to treat teachers with less respect than they deserve. Your classmates might be able to get away with this attitude, but you cannot. You need these teachers far more than your classmates do. They are the wizards who might possess the magic that unlocks learning. One of them (and which one is often unknowable) might have the magic to unlock learning for you. All of them can help you along the path if you can show them that you want to learn and that you honor them for trying to teach you. If choosing appropriate behavior is your difficulty, ask your teacher to become your partner in learning how to make better behavior choices. They will respect and encourage your efforts to replace negative behaviors with positive ones.

Parents

Educators today are often overworked and underappreciated. Your child, because of his or her unique learning style, is almost surely going to require more effort from a conscientious teacher than the other students in the class—and you are going to ask for more. The only bargaining chip you have to offer in return is genuine respect for a fine teaching professional and the chance for that teacher to make a true difference in a deserving student's life. These are not small chips. Good teachers will be motivated by them. Do whatever you can to show your genuine appreciation to dedicated teachers and to "help" your child be a deserving student. You can always model respect for your child's teachers and show your child how much you value education.

Educators

Some of these children are why you became teachers. Don't miss one. Be vigilant.

STRATEGY THREE
Working Harder and Longer

I t is a sad but unavoidable reality that nearly every academic task and many simple life activities take students with learning challenges longer to complete than their non-challenged peers. Most of these tasks require a more conscious effort as well. It is a major burden having a learning challenge and unfortunately it does not go away. I have always had to work longer and harder than most of my peers to achieve similar results. I know I will always have to do this and I must simply maintain the belief that my goals and dreams are worth the extra effort. Yet, I often resent the unfairness of the situation; I cannot deny that having learning challenges has a daily impact on my time and energy.

Every student with learning challenges who aspires to success must come to terms with this reality. They must come to accept that they will have to allow more time and devote more energy to accomplishing their dreams than their non-challenged peers. They must believe that their dreams are worth it. This is not an attitude easy to accept or to maintain. Those who advise the student with learning challenges can help tremendously by acknowledging and respecting the extra effort the student routinely expends. They can help tremendously by reinforcing that the student's dreams are worth the effort.

Social challenges can cause frustration, isolation and depression. A student of mine who had been diagnosed with Asperger's Syndrome once told me that he felt like an alien in a human body in a human world. He had been taught that he was supposed to be able to read social cues from facial expressions, tones of voice and body language. The meanings of smiles and frowns cross most human cultures. He simply didn't have that language. He had to learn it all by rote. Every time he looked at a person, he had to mentally review the facial expressions he had been taught and to match up the corresponding emotion to that expression on the face confronting him. You can imagine how exhausting and isolating it must have been to constantly misunderstand, be misunderstood and be marginalized.

Parents and teachers can compensate by creating scenarios for success and encouraging all improvements. They can recognize how energy-sapping social deficits can be and limit demands appropriately.

Many times I envied my friends who were able to blow off homework and papers until the last possible minute and still get a good grade. I had to work ten times harder and longer to get the same grade. Often my friends could go out during the week while I would be doing homework. Sometimes I got discouraged and resented my LD deficits, but when I put in the work and got an A, the high was definitely worth the effort! I felt proud of myself. Having to work harder and longer than others to achieve the same results might seem unfair, but the sooner you come to terms with it, the sooner you can move past it and on to success.

There are some strategies to help combat the extra time involved in doing certain tasks. Tutors and adaptive technology can both make the process a little faster, easier and less lonely. Many schools and colleges offer professional or peer tutoring free of charge or at a minimal cost. Often a retired teacher or others in the community will do volunteer tutoring. Organizations like Big Brothers or Big Sisters offer free mentors, and volunteers with special teaching skills might be requested. A good tutor can give invaluable encouragement and emotional support as well as academic expertise. Screen readers, books-on-tape, and dictation programs can save time and energy. I encourage students to use all these techniques whenever possible. Parents and educators must stay abreast of new technologies and community resources and make them available to their students as soon as possible.

Checklist for Strategy Three:

- The reality is that students with learning challenges must work harder and longer to achieve similar results to their peers.
- Social deficits can be additionally energy-sapping.
- Adaptive technologies can help close the gap.
- Tutors and mentors are an invaluable resource.

Especially for:

Students

Having a learning challenge is tough and while it might get easier, it probably won't go away. Your goals and dreams are worth the extra time and effort. They are yours and are special. Try to find some activity, sport or hobby that you love to balance your extra academic and social stressors. What you have to deal with is tough, but there are many who are dealing with tougher challenges. Try attending a Special Olympics event or volunteer at a children's cancer camp to restore your perspective.

Parents

Practically, you can help with time management, allowing the extra time needed to complete tasks without time crunches. Emotionally, you can validate your child's goals and dreams and celebrate progress and successes whenever possible. Your respect for the grit it takes to put in the extra effort goes a long way. Be vigilant; keep searching for time-saving technologies and strategies for your child. Regularly review your child's homework to insure that assigned tasks are appropriate and not excessively repetitive. Depending on your student's diagnosis you have the right to approach the teacher and to limit excessive assignments in the IEP accommodations page.

You can create socially positive experiences and activities for your child with learning and social challenges. There are many socially protected activities such as Big Sisters and Big Brothers where your child can be paired with an adult with the training to be an effective friend and mentor. You might have adult friends willing to take your child under their wings for mutually agreeable activities.

Encourage all self-esteem building and fun activities. For me, horseback riding was crucial for letting off steam and experiencing the close relationship with the animal. The fact that my riding instructor treated me as physically and emotionally "normal" and let me get away with nothing gave me a real sense of accomplishment. I use horses, ponies and other farm animals for esteem-building in therapy sessions. Many communities offer therapeutic horsemanship sessions which are fun and esteem-building for learning and social challenges as well as for physical challenges. Your child might enjoy art or music. It might seem that your child's schedule and yours are already overbooked with academics and other therapies. Find time for something they love and do all you can to encourage it.

ATTITUDE

<u>Educators</u>

Recognize the extra effort and time required to complete assignments and try to eliminate as much busywork as possible. Rote is great, but writing a spelling word 20 times might be only mildly irritating for most of your class, but for this child it might be excruciating and to no purpose. Keep in mind that for the student with learning challenges, too much practice of skills becomes counterproductive. When students are on overload, their brains "shut down;" then it is impossible for them to develop new skills. Please be sure that all assignments are necessary and meaningful for your student. Consider the possibility that the student would be able to learn the material by completing ten problems rather than 15 or 20.

STRATEGY FOUR
Planning Ahead

Organization, sequencing and time management: These are skills that many students with learning challenges find extremely difficult to master. These skills all take planning ahead, and planning ahead is the one skill that the students with learning challenges, and those who advise them, cannot do without. As I said in Strategy Three, almost everything the student with learning challenges does takes longer and requires more lead time than for their non-challenged peers. Students with learning challenges must always be planning for the future. They must always be laying the groundwork for the next step.

For example, if students take tests in a resource-room and use a reader, scribe or extended time, they must usually make arrangements for these accommodations a week before each test or exam. A review session with a tutor before a test is ideally scheduled three days in advance rather than the night before. Reading and writing assignments take longer too. With important writing assignments, doing an outline and first draft and submitting them to the teacher for approval might confirm that a student is on the right track and demonstrate to the teacher that the student truly cares.

If students are dependent on audio books or recorded handout materials to be successful in their courses, they must plan ahead to get those recordings as soon as they know which courses they will be taking. I found that this process can take several weeks to several months. At the college level, some schools provide early course enrollment as an accommodation to give a student more lead time. Be sure to ask a college if it can provide this for the student. Some very structured disability-support programs might guide a student through this process, but most likely it will be the student's responsibility as it was mine. This is a multi-step process and getting the current syllabus from a teacher or professor is just the beginning. At some colleges it might be possible to get lists of the textbooks from the bookstore, but a student will need to get handout materials from the teachers or professors themselves.

Below is an example of a letter of request I wrote to teachers or professors requesting their syllabi. Benefits of such a letter are that it will identify the student as serious and it will provide the student the chance to plan ahead. Be prepared to follow up with emails or phone calls a few days after sending these letters out. Few teachers or professors understand how time-consuming getting material taped can be. Few recognize how necessary it is to have a syllabus for the semester in place months in advance. Students with learning challenges, requiring audio books, will often need three months to order the book, receive it and forward it to Learning Ally to be taped and returned to you. Some colleges are now in the process of working with publishers to make downloadable Word or PDF files of texts available to students with disabilities that can be read aloud with a screen reading computer program. This will be a giant step forward for all of us! On the other hand, some colleges assign teaching staff to classes at the last minute and thus an accurate syllabus might not be available. Course catalogues often specify a particular professor or simply say "staff." If "staff" is indicated for a course you wish or need to take, I strongly suggest you contact disability-support services for advice before signing up for that class.

Nothing is worse for a student with a reading deficit than to begin a semester without the textbooks and handouts in an audio format. Being behind from the beginning almost ensures failure.

Having the ability to look at the syllabus ahead of time will also show the student how much commitment the class will entail. It is even useful for students who do not have reading difficulties to realize how heavy a load they will carry and take the time to begin to read during the summer or between semesters. Both in high school and in college, if writing is the challenge, it might be possible to balance courses with heavy writing and reading requirements with math courses or other courses that are required but less demanding, and vice-versa if math is the challenge. Another benefit is that the letter of request will identify the student as serious and able to plan ahead.

It is very sad that the students with learning challenges are the ones who have to be two steps ahead. Furthermore, many of them have huge organizational deficits and already spend a lot of time on any task. Always being two steps ahead, however, is the best way a student with learning challenges can ensure success.

Your name
Your address and phone number
Date
RE: AUDIO BOOKS
COURSE: (department and course number)

Dear Dr. X,

I am planning to take the above course with you this fall. I rely heavily on audio books because of my learning disability. I must order audio texts several months in advance to allow taping time if the book is not in stock.

I would be very grateful if you would send me a complete list of textbooks that you plan to use for the above course.

I would also be grateful for copies of any additional printed materials, including handouts that you plan to assign so I can arrange to have them taped.

If you are using only portions of any book, please note exactly which chapters or pages will be assigned. Because time is so short between semesters, my readers can record only the necessary portions.

ATTITUDE

Audio transcriptions require:

FOR BOOKS:

Title
Author
Publisher
Edition (critical)
Copyright Date
ISBN number

FOR OTHER PRINTED MATERIAL: a legible copy. I can pick up the list from your office, you can put it in the mail (your address) or you can e-mail it to me at (your e-mail address), whichever is most convenient for you. If you have any questions, I can be reached at (your phone number).

I sincerely appreciate this extra effort on your part and I look forward to being in your course this winter.

Sincerely,

(Your Name)

PLANNING AHEAD

Students with learning challenges need to plan ahead earlier for going to college. For example, other students can wait until junior year to investigate college choices. Many colleges with comprehensive programs that support students with learning challenges require extensive documentation and on-campus interviews which might need to be scheduled many months in advance. These programs almost always require two applications: one to the college and one to the support program. This doubles or triples the paperwork for the student with learning challenges. While many high schools have excellent college advisors, it is rare for advisors to know anything about the many excellent support programs for students with learning challenges. And they know even less about these colleges' unique application processes. Most of this research must be borne by the student, parents or a specialized college placement consultant—if you can find one. It is always a balancing act between available energy and available time. The student with learning challenges must actively plan for his or her own miracles.

So too must their parents and other mentors plot and plan for the future they hope for the student to attain. Constant reevaluation of competencies and skills and vigilance for new opportunities are needed to encourage the growth and stretch that makes success a real possibility.

ATTITUDE

Parents, as your student's advocate, you energetically seek out every social and academic "advantage" possible, but you must also be vigilant in guarding against the effects of "overprotection." Even if your child is very lucky and you find a good preparatory school or a school that offers a lot of support, beware, ironically these very programs that are such a crucial help to your child can also prevent your child from taking the next step they need to achieve academic independence.

For example, from age six to my sophomore year in high school, I attended private schools that were devoted to helping students with learning challenges. These schools clarified my strengths and weaknesses and helped me to come up with strategies which became the tools to pursue my further education. However, at the same time, they often wanted me to stay for "just another year or two" because they believed that I was "not quite ready" for a more competitive and less protective environment. After much anguished consideration, my parents and I decided that if I was ever going to have a chance to attend college I needed to build an academic record at a competitive high school. In spite of the professional's advice, we took the chance. As it turned out, it was the correct decision for me. My local public high school provided excellent LD support through a resource-room and extremely supportive teachers who, after they understood that I was a serious student, genuinely cared about and promoted my success. I flourished there and graduated with honors.

Looking back, I know that my private-school teachers really felt that they could help me more and, furthermore, did not want me to risk painful and discouraging failure. They believed that they knew best, and I believe they had my best interests in mind. On the other hand, if I had never dared, I would not have achieved as much as I did as quickly as I did.

Public school teachers, advisors and resource-room teachers can fall into the same overprotective mode. They are committed to their students professionally and emotionally too. They might be reluctant to risk failures by raising the bar and thus pass up opportunities a student needs for growth. This applies to choosing the difficulty level of courses throughout a student's academic career as well as how much time the student spends in "special" academic support programs. As advocates, it is important to guard against these potentially limiting tendencies. Know your rights and advocate for all the support your student needs, but also guard against over protectiveness, which can be just as crippling as too little support.

<u>Checklist for Strategy Four:</u>

- Plan, plan, plan ahead.

- Make any and all appointments early.

- Realize that some accommodations take months to get into place.

- Understand that most teachers don't realize how long the process takes.

- Acknowledge and work past your organizational issues.

- Guard against crippling overprotection.

- Constantly reassess progress; raise the academic and social bar as needed.

Especially for:

Students

Planning is everything. Do anything you can to strengthen your organizational and time-management skills. Work with a mentor, mother, father, tutor, whoever is organized and willing to help you daily to stay on top of scheduling and completing tasks. Learn to create and update a computer calendar as soon as possible. Put every assignment, test and deadline on it. Don't forget to schedule the fun things too!

Parents

If you are the least bit disorganized, find someone your child can count on to be their organizational mentor on a daily basis. This is probably the greatest skill you can give your child after potty training. Discover the steps needed to schedule accommodations such as audio books, and help your child learn to schedule them and to become independent with planning.

On a broader scale, it is important to remember that as your child gains new skills you must constantly reevaluate his or her academic and social environments to be sure that they remain challenging enough to continue to "stretch" your child while maintaining the supports that will provide all of the opportunities needed for success. After you achieve this environment for your child, it is so tempting to sigh with relief and relax in that safe harbor. Unfortunately, you must guard against resting at anchor too long and missing the signs that it is time to raise the hook and sail forward yet again. Always remember that students with academic and social challenges are running a race against time. They "started behind" with certain deficits and have catching up to do. Our educational system has a fairly finite timeline. Support services are not offered forever. Try to keep a wise sailor's weather eye on that timeline.

Educators

Consider being open to encouraging your students with learning challenges to submit outlines and rough drafts of important writing assignments in order to confirm that they are on task as you intend. Make your syllabi early and make them available to your students. Recognize how long lead times are and how desperately dependent on these services your students are. If students with learning challenges start your class without the materials they need, they are starting at a disadvantage. Guard against overprotection and encourage new challenges and growth. Be vigilant in seeking opportunities to "stretch" your students and encourage them to set goals and to celebrate achieving them.

ADVOCACY

STRATEGY FIVE
Acceptance

A lot of excellent material has been written about the critical importance of self-advocacy for the student with learning challenges. I am sure that all teachers would agree that it is a powerful tool for any student with learning challenges to have in his or her toolbox. The first prerequisite for effective self-advocacy is acceptance: acceptance of one's self and one's learning challenges.

Acceptance was easier for me than for most students with learning challenges, because I could point to a specific event, my aneurysm, which had "caused" my learning disability. There were no years of painfully mounting doubt nor any confusion about why I was different and learned differently, not for me nor for my parents and my educators. No one was to blame and certain facts could not be denied. For most students with learning challenges and their parents, achieving this acceptance is much more difficult. For many parents the diagnosis of a learning challenge—ADHD, Asperger's, autism or whatever the classification might be—comes as a crushing blow that threatens to destroy many of the hopes and dreams that they have imagined for this child. They might blame themselves or each other as the cause for the "damage." They might deny that the diagnosis is accurate. They might feel embarrassment and isolate themselves and their families from the help they need. Families might go through many of the stages that we associate with grieving as they come to grips with the implications for their child's education and future. This reaction is natural and necessary. It is also painful, energy-sapping and potentially isolating. If too extended, it can steal time and energy from the more important priority—seeking the remedial and compensatory environment required to ameliorate deficits and get on with learning and life.

Fortunately, there are many fine books written about coming to terms with a diagnosis of learning challenges. Also the Learning Disabilities Association (LDA[2]), Children and

---

[2] Learning Disabilities Association of America website www.ldanatl.org

Adults with Attention-Deficit/Hyperactivity Disorder (CHADD[3]), International Dyslexia Association (IDA[4]), Autism Speaks,[5] Aphasia Recovery Connection (ARC[6]), and other organizations have chapters in most communities with workshops and support groups dedicated to helping parents and siblings through this process. These groups are very valuable for networking and for gaining information regarding community resources available to parents of students with learning challenges.

It is crucial for students with learning challenges and their families to find ways to get over blame and denial. It wastes valuable energy. Please encourage the students with learning challenges you advise to do whatever it takes—support groups, extended personal or family counseling, spiritual discovery, whatever—to achieve acceptance. It is the first step to healing.

From the moment I woke up partially paralyzed and unable to speak, in the hospital, at the age of six, I realized that I could not waste time focusing on why this had happened to me. Being so young probably made me more accepting of my new circumstances. There were times when I melted down in

---

[3]CHADD www.chadd.org
[4] IDA www.interdys.org
[5] Autism Speaks www.autismspeaks.org
[6] ARC www.aphasiarecoveryconnection.org

frustration at things I could no longer do, such as talk and remember words. But in calmer moments I came to the realization that the only way to succeed was to think positively about where I could go from there. But the only way for students with learning challenges to get here from there is to be able to first accept and then understand that they have a learning challenge.

After acceptance comes the understanding and the ability to clearly explain your learning challenge to others. Being able to explain that you have learning challenges does not mean you have to introduce yourself with it, as if it is part of your name! I mean only that you should be able to explain your learning style and accommodation needs to the appropriate people at the appropriate times to get the appropriate help you need to succeed.

Checklist for Strategy Five:

- It is important to accept and understand your individual learning challenge.
- If necessary, find counseling or whatever help you might need to achieve acceptance.
- It is important to be able to explain your learning style and accommodation needs to others.

Especially for:

Students

For many students the diagnosis of a learning challenge comes after an extended time of frustration trying to learn the way most of their peers do and confusion about why they can't seem to do what others find so seemingly easy. By the time testing is done and someone explains what is going on or not going on in their brains, they have begun to feel discouraged, different and might have been teased and called dumb. It has been a painful and damaging process. A diagnosis might come as a relief because now at least there is something with a name that can be definitely treated. For some, a diagnosis might frighten more than it relieves. Either way, the diagnosis of a learning challenge eventually means a lot of hard work and a struggle to achieve goals that were considered easy reaches in the past. Appropriate school interventions will reduce much of the stress of past academic failures, and effective learning strategies will enable successes. But still, a learning difference is a paradigm shift and takes a lot of getting used to and becoming reconciled to. There might be loss and hope and fear of the unknown. Counseling might help and time will be needed to come to terms with what might lie ahead. It will certainly take time to understand the mechanics of "how" you learn differently, and it will take time to gain the skill and the composure to explain these learning needs to others. Acceptance will be an ongoing, lifelong task. But it is important to waste as little energy on blame or "Why me?" as possible. Try to save that precious energy for the tasks ahead. You will find it more rewarding. And don't forget that a diagnosis is not a prognosis for failure; just the opposite—it can be the beginning to the path to success.

Parents

There is a great deal more understood about the brain and the various learning challenges than there was when my parents and I were beginning to cope with my learning issues. Even so, most parents have experienced the same doubt-ridden and emotionally tumultuous ride that their child has before receiving an enlightening diagnosis. Denial, they say, is not just a river in Africa. And hundreds of books and pamphlets have been written to help parents work through and move past denial when their child is diagnosed with a learning difference. Parents cause untold anguish blaming themselves, each other, genetics, God—anyone—for the changed paradigm they face. The more quickly they can learn about their child's learning style and needs and the more quickly they avail themselves of the help they need, the sooner they will be able to be a reliable support for their child. LDA of America has chapters in hundreds of communities throughout the world dedicated to helping parents understand, cope and choose services for their child with learning differences. Similar, dedicated support organizations are available for those with Asperger's, autism, aphasia and ADHD. Seek support with one of these resources and/or arrange for family counseling with an experienced professional as soon as you receive the diagnosis. The time and treasure spent now will pay huge dividends for your child.

Educators

It is to be hoped that your professional training will help you to recognize the various levels of acceptance and understanding of learning differences evidenced by both your students and their parents. You can play a major role in facilitating the appropriate support and services for parents and students new to coping with a learning challenge. It will be a great gift to them. The other issue is acceptance, awareness and understanding from the rest of the classmates. My undergraduate service learning project involved the design and implementation of a seven-week curriculum for "Demystification of Learning Differences" for a sixth-grade class. It was an eye-opening experience. There are many resources available should your class or playground need a little sensitizing. All students benefit when they learn about and accept individual differences of any type. After all, our differences are what make each one of us a unique individual.

STRATEGY SIX
Self-knowledge and Articulating It

If acceptance of having a learning challenge is the first prerequisite for effective self-advocacy, the second is to gain a clear understanding of one's own learning challenge. Everyone's learning challenges are unique. Students with learning challenges must learn at least enough about their learning challenges to know what accommodations they need to perform well. Students should be able to explain the reasons for those accommodations to teachers, as well as to anyone else who needs to know.

Acquiring this knowledge is not easy. It involves complex issues. Articulating this knowledge to others is also a difficult and potentially emotional task. It is probably best approached on a gradual and cumulative basis. Many students with learning challenges benefit from participating in meetings during which the results of their assessment testing are explained to their parents.

Whether administered by an independent specialist or by your local school district, you should meet with the tester for an explanation of the test results. He or she should explain the reports and discuss how they translate into daily school and life tasks. Be sure you spend all the time you need with the tester to fully understand your student's strengths and deficits. It might be helpful for both the student and parents together to spend some time with the specialist. Know that you have the right to bring another professional or family member to any academic or medical conference, evaluation or meeting. It is often useful to have two or more people absorbing complicated and emotional information. Making notes of questions and goals before a meeting is very helpful. Do not feel intimidated by the vocabulary used or be shy about asking for clarification of anything you do not understand. These are complex and nuanced issues and you have both the right and the responsibility to clear understanding—as does your student. Your goal here is to come out of this meeting with an understanding of how your student learns best and what accommodations he or she needs in order to learn.

Many students with learning challenges often benefit from participating in their Individualized Education Program[7] (IEP) conferences to make sure the goals and accommodations decided on make sense to them. The same goes for parent-teacher conferences. Each is an opportunity for students to learn more about their unique process of learning. The bottom line is that it is the student's own brain and students with learning challenges must learn how it works.

After they have a grasp of their learning styles and accommodation needs, it is a useful strategy to practice and role play communicating this information to others in depth. This can be done in detail for a new teacher and in more general terms, for example, for a new scoutmaster or soccer coach. The ability to discuss one's needs, knowledgeably and unemotionally, is immensely empowering. Acceptance and self-knowledge can carry students with learning challenges many miles on their paths toward their "possibilities."

As I discussed in Strategy Two, there will be teachers and others that the student will encounter who might not

---

[7] IEP: Individualized Education Program is the legal document that defines a child's special education program. It includes the disability under which the child qualifies for Special Education Services, the services the school will provide, yearly goals and objectives, and any accommodations that must be made to assist learning.

acknowledge learning challenges or who are very uninformed about specific needs and accommodations. Sometimes teachers simply have bad days and behave imprudently. While these situations are frustrating and difficult to resolve, students with learning challenges are much better off if they can unemotionally explain their learning strengths, weaknesses and accommodation needs.

Sometimes it is just impossible for the student to resolve an accommodation issue with a teacher on his or her own. In high school, I had an English teacher who gave a pop quiz one day, around mid-semester. At that time, my accommodations included having tests read to me in the resource-room and we had been doing that for scheduled tests and pop quizzes up to that point. That day he simply lost his temper and insisted that I take the quiz in the classroom. He began to get loud and abusive, embarrassing me in front of the other students. I excused myself and went to the resource-room teacher. When the resource-room teacher confronted him, he was rude to her too. It was ultimately resolved by the principal. The teacher apologized to me a couple of days later and we finished the semester without further incident and on reasonable terms. In cases like that, it is helpful for the student to know when to disengage politely and seek help from another authority. Role playing would be ideal here.

SELF-KNOWLEDGE AND ARTICULATING IT

Self-knowledge about one's learning difference and the ability to articulate basic information about it are valuable tools to have in one's tool kit.

Checklist for Strategy Six:

- Students with learning challenges must be able to explain their learning differences to others, including teachers and other advocates who will need to understand it.

- Students must be able to explain their learning challenges without becoming emotional.

- Role playing hypothetical scenarios can be valuable experiences to help with this.

- Students should be involved with their assessments to help them understand their strengths and weaknesses.

- Students should be allowed to participate in their IEP meetings.

- Not everyone will understand right away. Patience is necessary when engaging with those not familiar with learning challenges.

Especially for:

Students

It can be embarrassing to have to explain to someone why you can't do what most of your friends do so easily. In your life there will be hundreds of situations in addition to school that require reading—the rules at a public pool or the handout at soccer practice. You will need or want to participate in these types of events, and you just can't let your embarrassment cheat you out of fun activities. Take the time to role play explaining your needs to others until you can do it clearly and without the pain of embarrassment. The accommodations you need are your legal rights. Many people with learning challenges who came before you have worked very hard to win these rights for you so that you can enjoy a full life in spite of your learning challenges. Take advantage of your rights.

Parents

Do help your children with the process of understanding their learning challenge. Invite your children to participate in testing evaluation meetings, IEPs and teacher conferences whenever it is appropriate and discuss what was learned after the sessions. You can start with just partial participation when the child is young and increase as appropriate. Help your children to articulate their needs without belligerence or embarrassment. Practice with your children at as young an age as possible, and "set up" opportunities to practice with pre-prepared professionals such as teachers and youth activities personnel. The ability to advocate for oneself will set a child apart from others, gain the respect of professionals, and be the first step to true independence.

Educators

Do take the extra time and effort to include students in their IEPs and evaluation reviews. They truly must understand how they learn and how they do not learn. Take the time to role play with them in self-advocacy skills. Take extra time to work with your socially challenged students so they too can learn to clarify their needs in a way that gains them the respect and cooperation they deserve. Practicing scripts in a safe environment will provide them the opportunity to develop the skills they need to become successful self-advocates.

STRATEGY SEVEN
Marketing Yourself/Creating the
Right Identity

How can students with learning challenges make their teachers view them as students worthy of their teachers' best efforts? How can students with learning challenges compel their teachers to recognize their unique "possibilities"? The student with learning challenges must make a conscious effort to differentiate himself or herself from all those other students competing for that teacher's skills and energy. Students with learning challenges need to recognize that just like a product in the marketplace, they need a "marketing plan" to enable them to stand out as an exceptional student. They can accomplish this by using a variety of "niche marketing" strategies to create and show case their unique identity.

ADVOCACY

Step one, "product differentiation," has been accomplished for most students with learning challenges before the first day of class. Upon receiving the student's diagnosis and documentation files, most teachers accept that the student with learning challenges is different from the majority of their students—they recognize that these students learn differently. Unfortunately, along with that recognition comes awareness that this student will require more creativity, time, effort and perhaps more paperwork than any of the rest of the students. Some teachers might meet this as an intriguing challenge and some might simply groan at the added burden. The critical step for the student with learning challenges is to create a positive identity as an exceptionally worthy student, albeit with learning challenges. This means marketing oneself as deserving of the teacher's extra effort.

Unfortunately, many teachers have either preconceived notions of, or actual experience with, students who use their diagnosis of learning challenges as crutches and excuses to avoid assignments. Former students might have put off mentioning their learning challenges until they are significantly behind in class, thus requiring a great deal of extra help from the teacher to catch up. Serious students with learning challenges definitely need to avoid getting caught up in this negative stereotype. They must devise strategies to present themselves as students who are highly motivated to learn and to succeed in school. They must demonstrate to their teachers that they are willing to go the extra mile or ten to reach their goals. This kind of "product advertising" works for goods in the marketplace and will work for the students with learning challenges throughout their educational careers—as long as they are sincere about their efforts to live up to their advertising claims. Let me share, in the next few sections, some of the specific "marketing strategies" that have worked for me.

<u>Checklist for Strategy Seven:</u>

- A teacher is an advocate that students need on their side.
- Students must market themselves as eager learners.
- Don't wait until the last minute to ask for help.
- Good students with learning challenges can turn negative stereotypes around.

Especially for:

Students

You are hoping for something "extra" from your teachers in your struggle to succeed. You need extra creativity, extra insight, extra time, extra something from your teachers to compensate for your learning challenges. In order to get that something extra, you really have to demonstrate to your teachers that you are worthy of their extra efforts. You have to find ways to show them that you truly care about learning what they are trying to teach and demonstrate that you are willing to put in the extra effort to make that learning possible. Most teachers will respect your sincere efforts and willingly respond with whatever extra skills and energy they have as long as they see you are sincere about learning. Realize that teachers went to school for a long time to teach, so learning and shaping young minds are important to them; if you show a sincere interest in learning, most teachers will respond positively.

Parents

Help your children to understand why they need each teacher's best efforts. Help them understand that they are truly worthy of each teacher's best. Help them seek and practice creative ways to ask for that help. Help them to seek and practice creative ways to show each teacher that they are worthy of that extra help. Help your children see that they are entering into a "contract" with each of their teachers. They are promising "I will do my very best if you will give me your very best."

Educators

Your students with learning challenges are among the students whose lives you can affect the most. Keep alert to the ones who can benefit from your best efforts. These students often walk a thin line between lives of productive independence and happiness and lives full of tragedy and despair for themselves and society. Try to nudge them toward the positive outcomes when it is within your power to do so.

STRATEGY EIGHT
Writing "The Letter"

A "self-marketing" strategy I found very effective both in high school and in college is the "introductory letter." I create a form letter suitable for every new teacher or professor and I personally give it to them the first day of the course. The letter introduces me both as a student with learning challenges and as a person. It tells them about my specific needs as a student with learning challenges: What accommodations I need, and why those accommodations will help me perform well in the instructor's course. It tells them about my goals, hopes and dreams. It tells them what I have accomplished so far, and what difficulties I have overcome. It implies that I am willing to work harder than most students to succeed in their course. It recognizes that my accommodations might cause them extra inconvenience and it invites them to be a critical partner in my pathway to my dreams. At the end of the letter, I offer to meet with the teacher to answer any questions he or she has about me or my accommodations. In high school, I attached a copy of the accommodations portion of my IEP to the letter.

There are several very practical reasons for this letter.

First: The teacher might or might not have studied the student's learning challenges documentation or IEP in depth. The letter might motivate the teacher to review the student's file and give some additional thought to how best to teach that student.

Second: Putting a face to an anonymous file is helpful to both teacher and student, especially if the student is one of 20 or 30 new faces.

Third: The letter is a written record of specific expectations for accommodations for a course, and any misunderstandings or questions about the instructor's implementation can be addressed early in the semester.

Fourth: The letter opens the line of communication between student and teacher in an inviting and non-threatening way.

WRITING "THE LETTER"

I have found several less tangible but equally valuable benefits:

First: The letter identifies students as individuals who do not wait for failure or trouble before they play the disability card. This matters a lot to some teachers. In my experience, many teachers have the perception that many of their students with learning challenges use their diagnosis as a crutch only after failure and, furthermore, they use it too late for a practical solution to be implemented. This results in frustration for both student and teacher.

Second: The letter presents a goal-oriented and motivated student.

Third: It presents a real person with hopes and dreams yet with past difficulties that had to be overcome.

Fourth: It invites a "partnership" in learning between the student and the teacher—an invitation that is not often formally extended by a student.

After presenting the letter, students should be willing to meet with the teacher if he or she requests a meeting. Students should be prepared to answer questions about their learning challenges, learning styles and accommodations. They should be prepared to work out the nuts and bolts of accommodation implementation. This is where role playing can be especially useful. If the teacher does not request a meeting, the student need not force one. The student can just ask politely, a few days later, if the teacher has any questions. The meeting itself is often not necessary. The letter has opened positive lines of communication.

I have found this letter to be a powerful tool. However, it is most important that students with learning challenges recognize and respect that this letter is an explicit contract between themselves and their teacher. It is the students' promise that they will do their best in return for the teacher's best—and it is critical for students to live up to this promise.

WRITING "THE LETTER"

Your name
Your address and phone number
Date
CLASS: (department and class number)

I would like to take a few moments to tell you a little about myself and to explain why I need the accommodations I am requesting in your course. (See attached IEP.)

(Here, talk about your history/accomplishments.) For example: In third grade I was diagnosed with a cluster of learning disabilities that impact my ability to read and process the written word. I attended XYZ Preparatory School in XYZ, until this year. XYZ is a prep school dedicated to empowering students with learning disabilities. I have worked hard to understand my learning disabilities and to develop specific strategies to compensate for them. I am looking forward to my first year at ABC High School as the next step in my academic career. I love learning and exposure to new ideas. I am organized, motivated, hard-working, and am totally serious about my studies. My hope is to attend DEF College which my father attended. My dream is to become a teacher of history. (Or state whatever positive characteristics and hopes and dreams you believe you have.)

ADVOCACY

Unfortunately, I still need a number of accommodations to help me learn and to help you measure accurately what I have actually learned. The aids I use outside of class are: subject area tutoring, audio books, a computer reading scanner for typed materials not available on tape, a reader for poor-quality printed material that won't scan, and a computer voice recognition dictation program. I rely heavily on "spell check" and word processing for as much of my work as I can. When I am pressed for time, I dictate to a scribe.

Accommodations I am requesting in your course are:

AUDIO BOOKS
Accurate and timely syllabi for texts, all handouts and outside reading assignments.

The MOST critical accommodation for me is acquiring a complete syllabus two or three months before a course so I have adequate time to order any material that is not currently available on audio. I rely heavily on audio of all printed material. These processes can take several months' lead time. My backup is a scanner; however the scanning process is time-consuming and if handouts are of poor quality, my scanner can't process them at all and I need to arrange for someone to read them to me.

EXAMS AND QUIZZES

Extended time for tests

Quiet testing area

Tests taped or read to me by a proctor

I can read, but it is still such a difficult process that I can lose the exact meaning of a question. By reading along with the proctor (or a tape), I can be sure of clearly understanding what your test questions are asking. The reason for requesting extended time is that working with a reader, tape or scribe simply takes longer.

PEER NOTE-TAKERS

In some classes, the process of writing and spelling is so difficult and time consuming that I cannot observe what the teacher is demonstrating on the board. Peer notes free me up to concentrate fully on what the teacher is presenting. I usually transcribe peer notes outside of class.

SCRIBING

Some exams and quizzes

Some written assignments

If I dictate, I can often be more creative and organize my thoughts better and save a great deal of time.

READING ALOUD

I prefer not to be asked to read aloud in class because I still stumble over many words. I like to actively participate in class in other ways.

(List whatever accommodations you need to succeed and explain why you need them and how they help you learn.)

My reading rate is improving and I am working hard to reduce my need for these accommodations. I appreciate your willingness to help me work around my learning disability and I understand that it takes extra effort on your part as well as on mine.

Thank you for taking the time to read this. I hope it will help you to understand a bit better how and why I use some of the accommodations I am requesting and that it will help you help me to achieve my goals in your course this year. If there is anything I can explain further, please ask me at any time.

Sincerely,

(Your Name)

<u>Checklist for Strategy Eight:</u>

- This letter should contain a description of your learning challenges, your accommodation needs, and more personal things like hopes and dreams.

- Prepare for a meeting afterwards if the teacher requests it.

- Role playing can be a great opportunity to prepare for this meeting.

- This letter is a contract. If you present this letter, you as the student must hold up your end of the bargain.

- This letter helps familiarize the teacher with the student's file, puts a face on the student, provides a written record, and opens communication lines between student and teacher.

- This letter also provides goals, presents the student as motivated and a real person, and opens a partnership between teacher and student.

Especially for:

Students

This letter is powerful. It does make an impact on most teachers and professors. Please do not use this letter unless you plan to do your best in this course. It is a promise to the teacher that you must honor. If you blow it off, and thus break trust with this teacher or professor, you will be making the future more difficult for other students with learning challenges who encounter this professor. If you are sincere in your promise, do take the time to role play a meeting. Most of the time professors never ask, but it is essential to be prepared when one does. Don't be threatened by a meeting. Be flattered. Interpret it as the teacher showing a genuine interest in you and be prepared to answer questions. The meeting might be the beginning of a valuable partnership.

Students with social or organizational challenges or ADHD and similar behavioral challenges need to be especially frank about their deficits and promise only behaviors that they think they can deliver. Teachers should appreciate intent and effort and respect an approximation of success.

Parents

This letter does have huge impact on some teachers and professors. Do impress on your student how important the implied promise is. Make sure they sincerely mean to live up to it. They are asking for trust. As parents, this is an opportunity to impress upon them the importance of keeping (or at least intending to keep) their word. Honesty will take them far.

Educators

While, as presented, this strategy might seem to you to be somewhat manipulative, it really can be an act of trust by the student and a promise of intended performance. It does give you an invitation to have a dialogue with the student before possible academic or accommodation issues hinder open communication. It shouldn't take you long to discern the sincerity of the writer, and should the student prove genuine, you might have the chance to get to know (and assist) an exceptional student. Try to take the time to explore.

STRATEGY NINE
Keeping the Promise

With the letter in the preceding strategy, the student has promised teachers to do his or her best, but what is the student's best? Naturally that depends upon each individual's academic, organizational, behavioral, motivational and social/interpersonal skills. However, there are some basic techniques that are universal and can be targeted, learned and set as goals. These have worked for me, and can make students, learning challenged or not, stand out positively in their classes.

Showing Respect

All students with learning challenges (or those without) can show that they respect their teachers both as fellow human beings and as dedicated professionals. They can make conscious efforts to be unfailingly polite and friendly in every encounter with a teacher, both in and out of class. They can set a goal to say "Hello" or "Good morning, Mr. X" with a friendly smile in every encounter with the teacher. This is simple good manners. Surprisingly, few students consistently make this effort and over time it does make a difference. You might not particularly like a teacher, but I am not asking you to develop a friendship, only to show respect. You won't have any one teacher for a very long time, but how each teacher responds to you and assists you will make a difference. If you do not get along with a teacher, your grade can be affected, but the teacher's job won't be affected; you will just seem like one more student who doesn't care.

Punctuality

Students with learning challenges can show that they value teachers' time by making an effort to be on time to class and for appointments. If their organizational deficits make punctuality difficult, then that should be addressed in their "letter." In this way, the teacher will know that it is an area in which the student is working to improve. A simple acknowledgment of the inconvenience with a sincere apology, instead of an excuse, is very effective when the student is late.

Homework

The student with learning challenges can make every effort to get every homework assignment in on time. There are a variety of time management and assignment-tracking strategies available to students with learning challenges. The recognition that more time and more effort need to be planned is the essential part of this effort. If you know you are going to need extra time to complete an assignment, ask for the time when the task is assigned. Don't wait until the assignment is late. This will show the teacher that you care about completing assignments.

Rough Drafts

A strategy that I found especially helpful on longer term assignments was the utilization of rough drafts. I request permission to bring rough drafts of work to my teachers for advice and suggestions for improvement well before the assignment is due. My high school's English department used rewrites extensively. All students had to submit work in progress at various stages before handing it in for a final grade. Many students just knocked out haphazard work in progress and then relied on their talent to do a final product the last night before the assignment deadline. I tried my best on the initial submission and used my teacher's time to truly improve my best efforts. Believe me, they knew the difference. While my final product might not have been better than or as good as some of my more talented peers, the teachers recognized that I was making a sincere effort to improve my skills. I have used this strategy to good effect in courses without rewrite policies. Some professors initially think I am somewhat compulsive, but they come to respect the effort. This strategy has saved me from expending a lot of energy on a misunderstood assignment as well. Now, as a college instructor, I use this strategy with all my students.

Extra Credit

Another strategy I have used to good effect in some courses is extra-credit. In areas that I knew my test-taking skills were likely to produce a poor assessment of what I had actually mastered, I asked for extra-credit assignments throughout the semester. If a student's test-taking skills are below average, he or she will need this edge to get good grades. The key is that the student must recognize that this strategy will be necessary and plan time for the extra work. He or she cannot wait until the end of the semester to implement it. This strategy does not work with all teachers. Some teachers simply do not believe that extra-credit should mitigate testing in any way. But even if the teacher does not extend the opportunity for extra-credit, the teacher does usually recognize that the student was willing to make the extra effort and that never hurts.

Class Participation

Most students with learning challenges must consciously plan ahead to participate in classes in a positive way. A strategy I used was preparing one insightful question about the homework reading material for each class, hoping that there would be an appropriate time in class to use it. The question demonstrated that I had done the reading assignment and, over time, my teachers realized that I cared about their course. Developing these questions was a good learning strategy for me as well.

Classroom Behavior

Students with attention deficit hyperactivity disorder (ADHD)[8] and other behavior challenges can have a difficult time controlling their classroom behavior. However, when they fail, they can make a point of apologizing to the teacher as soon as possible after class.

The bottom line of all these strategies is to actively demonstrate that these students with learning challenges are

---

[8] Attention-deficit/hyperactivity disorder (AD/HD) is a neurobiological disorder. It is characterized by developmentally inappropriate impulsivity, inattention, and in some cases, hyperactivity.

making a sincere effort to keep their promise to do their very best. To the extent that any of these behaviors are outstanding as compared to other classmates, these students will have succeeded in standing out in a positive fashion and in differentiating themselves as exceptionally motivated students.

Students with learning challenges must strive to enable their teachers to see these student's "possibilities" in a new light. There is no more powerful ally than a teacher who truly believes in a student. Teachers became teachers because they wanted to make a positive difference in young peoples' lives. They did not choose to become teachers for the money or because they believed that the world would be a better place if everyone in it was exposed to eighth-grade algebra (well, there might be a couple of them). Students with learning challenges can extend to their teachers a unique invitation to achieve their most cherished teaching goals through these challenged and challenging students. Teachers experience too many students who take their teachers for granted and do not seem to care whether they learn or not. By showing that they are truly committed to learning, students with learning challenges can touch a basic nerve in many fine teachers.

Checklist for Strategy Nine:

- Basic techniques and strategies can help students achieve and demonstrate their personal best.

- It is vital to be punctual, courteous, and kind in the classroom.

- Do all homework and plan on the time it will take to complete.

- Utilize rough drafts to help teachers appreciate the work in progress.

- Asking for extra credit can help, even when teachers don't give any.

- Participation is very important. Plan for quality participation.

- Behavior-challenged students need to acknowledge and apologize to the teacher for any inappropriate behaviors as soon as possible.

Especially for:

The Student

Take the time to brainstorm, list and set as goals specific behaviors that will demonstrate your efforts to do your very best. Keep a journal of successful behaviors and repeat them often. Record failures and brainstorm with a mentor on how to avoid them in the future. Review your goals periodically and reset them as needed. No one expects perfection, least of all teachers. Most everyone respects effort and improvement. You should respect and celebrate your improvements too.

Parents

Help your student to brainstorm, list and set appropriate goals to demonstrate and document his or her genuine efforts and accomplishments. Acts that begin as "rote" assignments can develop into positive and productive habits. A journal of the accomplishment of short-term or long-term goals can become a proof of progress and a document to celebrate with joy. Help your student to recognize and celebrate his or her progress and improvement in "keeping the promise" to do their very best.

Educators

Help your students with learning challenges to develop and implement simple strategies for positive behaviors both academically and socially. Try to find creative ways for them to demonstrate their mastery of academic material. Try to be flexible with format and design of assignments and tests. Help them set realistic behavioral and organizational goals and acknowledge their incremental improvements. Help them to see instances of both success and failure as "learning" opportunities to be valued and taken advantage of. Effort is laudable, but improvement and accomplishment is the payoff. Help them create legitimate successes to celebrate. Please don't expect perfection; all students have bad days, so accept bad days from students with learning challenges. Encourage them to try again.

STRATEGY TEN

The Evaluation Questionnaire

Whenever I completed a course in high school, my mother sent a questionnaire to my teachers with a letter asking them to evaluate a variety of my skills they might have observed in their classes. It also asked for their advice on ways for me to improve a variety of skills and behaviors based on their experience with me as a student. The letter thanked the teachers for any extra effort with accommodations, for encouraging me throughout the year and for being a good teacher. Without exception, teachers were willing to return these questionnaires, and many of their comments were extremely helpful to me. The letters demonstrated that the family valued the teacher's opinion, and the student was making an effort to improve her academic behavior. The completed questionnaires also provided an excellent indication of which teachers to ask to write college-recommendation letters a couple of years later. (I suspect that this might have been my mother's primary motivation all along.) Copies of the questionnaires could also serve as refreshers for teachers willing to write recommendations, but who had not had me in a course for a year or two. Their comments were very helpful to me in setting goals for improvement, and I think such comments might be helpful to other students too.

Sample Evaluation Letter to Teachers
Parent Name
Parent Address
Parent Telephone Number

Date

Name of Teacher

Teacher's Address

Or High School Address

Dear Mr./Mrs. (Name of Teacher),

I know how much (Name of Student) appreciated your instruction, support and encouragement throughout this past (quarter, semester, year), as well as your understanding of his/her learning disability. He/She enjoyed your course immensely. As his/her parent I want to SINCERELY thank you and also to ask one further favor.

This was (Name of Student's) first year at (Name of High School) and her first year at a school not specifically devoted to students with learning disabilities. Thanks in great part to teachers like you, it has been a successful transition and we are very pleased and proud of the work (Name of Student) has accomplished.

ADVOCACY

He/She strongly desires to attend college and at this point is interested in a degree in (Degree Interest). Fortunately, there are a number of colleges with comprehensive LD support programs and I am trying to gain practical knowledge of his/her specific academic strengths and weaknesses in order to prepare him/her for college demands and to match him/her up with the program that will give him/her the greatest opportunity for success.

I would be very grateful if you would take a few minutes of your time to share your candid assessment of him/her as a student over the past quarter/semester and to give me any of your insights that would help us in planning his/her academic future.

1) I think it would be particularly helpful for us to understand:

His/her general strengths as a student?

_____

_____

_____

THE EVALUATION QUESTIONNAIRE

Your suggestions of what he/she or his/her parents could do to build on them?

_____

_____

_____

His/her specific weaknesses as a student?

_____

_____

_____

Any specific steps you feel he/she or his/her parents could do over the next year and a half to compensate for weaknesses or remediate them?

_____

_____

_____

2) Please touch on some of the following that strike you as particularly important:

His/her attitude, motivation?

_____

_____

_____

ADVOCACY

His/her ability to seek help needed appropriately?

_____

_____

_____

His/her ability to work independently?

_____

_____

_____

His/her ability to cope with criticism, setbacks, etc.?

_____

_____

_____

His/her organizational skills?

_____

_____

_____

How he/she coped with the normal workload?

_____

_____

_____

THE EVALUATION QUESTIONNAIRE

How much and what kind of extra support he/she
required of you in class?

_____

_____

_____

How much and what kind of extra support he/she
required of you outside of class?

_____

_____

_____

How he/she handled class participation?

_____

_____

_____

How he/she handled the homework load?

_____

_____

_____

Information that you did not have about (Name of Student) that would have been useful for you to have before teaching (Name of Student) or think would be useful to future teachers?

_____

_____

_____

Would you be comfortable writing a college letter of recommendation for (Name of Student) in the future?

_____

_____

_____

I know this is a lot to ask of you in the middle of a busy school year (or during your busy summer), but it would be enormously valuable to us for planning (Name for Student's) future.

Sincerely,

(Name of Parent)

Note: Include a self-addressed stamped envelope and write a thank you note to any teacher who takes the time to send you a response—even if you are not thrilled with the content.

Checklist for Strategy Ten:

- A questionnaire can be invaluable for finding the student's strengths and weaknesses.

- The questionnaire can be used to show what areas need improvement in the future.

- It can also be used to find teachers for college recommendations and to refresh those teachers' memories of the student several years later.

- A questionnaire demonstrates that a family is serious about education and respects teacher's assessments.

Especially for:

<u>Students</u>

You might not like everything a teacher writes about you and your academic skills, but might gain some really useful ideas for areas needing improvement. If you have any of those teachers again for another course, you will have new insight about what they value and don't like. On the other hand, you might get an unexpected compliment or two as well.

<u>Parents</u>

Teachers aren't too likely to put too much negative information on paper that they have not already addressed in student conferences with you. Still, they might have useful suggestions for remedial work and behavior modifications that you can use as strategies for next semester or year. They might say some very nice things about your child that you will be thrilled to share and celebrate with your child. In any case you have gained insight on which teachers you can count on for recommendations, and they certainly know you care about your child's education. Also, teachers obviously talk with one another, so even if your student does not take another course with the teacher who completed the questionnaire, it is most likely that this teacher has told others about your strong support for your child and also for the teacher. Teachers almost always appreciate supportive parents.

Educators

This is extra work. Your comments are on paper and could conceivably come back to haunt you. Your school might have policies about this kind of request. Still, it is from a parent who clearly cares, and completing the questionnaire provides an opportunity to be tactfully candid about the student's attitude and abilities. If you have anything positive to say, know that the student (and parents) will greatly appreciate your praise. If you have constructive criticisms or concrete suggestions for improvement it would be a real kindness to offer them. Be as candid as you can.

STRATEGY ELEVEN

Accommodations: Helping Students with Learning Challenges to Do It Themselves

Accommodations are often crucial to students' academic success. They certainly were to mine. I used readers, scribes, extended test time, audio books, note-takers and tutors. To obtain these accommodations often requires much organization, planning, and scheduling. It is a tragic irony that implementing the very accommodations that enable success can add significantly to these students' burdens. For this reason, in many schools, teachers and resource-rooms will do most of this planning and scheduling for their students with learning challenges. Many resource-room teachers actually prefer to arrange accommodations for their students rather than take the time to teach them how to do it for themselves. Many parents believe that arranging accommodations for their child is one way of lightening their child's academic burden. I believe that these are short-term views, which in the long run seriously limits the student's "possibilities."

Students with learning challenges do not benefit from being dependent on others for their critical needs. They should be taught to make their own accommodation arrangements. Of course no one can do it all at once. It must be a gradual process and initially practiced with real safety nets in place. But if students and those who advise them make independence a joint goal, it can be achieved. Over time, students with learning challenges can learn to schedule those readers and special test times. They can offer to pick up tests and take them to the resource-room (tests can be placed in sealed envelopes). If students with learning challenges use audio materials, they can gradually take responsibility for getting the list of texts and outside reading from their teachers. They can learn how to order the audio material from the various audio sources themselves.

I encourage students with learning challenges to make it their goal to achieve complete independence in securing the academic accommodations needed in order to succeed by the beginning of their senior year in high school. I urge those who advise students with learning challenges to take the extra time to teach their students to gradually take over these crucial tasks. I urge these advisors to devise ways to empower their students to meet this goal. Independence is energizing. It is worth the struggle.

Checklist for Strategy Eleven:

- Independence in arranging for accommodations is the ultimate goal.

- Independence in arranging accommodations should be a goal to be completed by the beginning of a student's senior year.

Especially for:

Students

It is worth it. It really is. Not depending on others to arrange your accommodations will set you free. You will be light-years ahead of peers in any post-graduate program.

Parents

The gift of independence is one of the greatest gifts that you can give. Arranging for accommodations is time-consuming for the student (as you know only too well) and safety nets are essential throughout the hand-over process, but the payoff in self-esteem is immense. You might have push back from the resource-room teacher or whoever at school arranges accommodations, but you should be able to make him or her see the advantages of fostering independence. If you have problems with the educators accepting your desire for your child to gain these skills, I suggest you make "accommodations independence" one of your child's major IEP goals for senior year of high school. The law is on your side.

Educators

It is very easy to fall into the trap of enabling dependence when it comes to arranging accommodations. Doing it yourself is easier, less time-consuming, you know it's done and done correctly, and besides, students have so much else on their plates. Don't do it. Take the extra time to work out a schedule to develop independence. You know the saying: "If you give a person a fish, he has food for a day; if you teach him how to fish, he has food for life." Teach your students skills for life. This is a clear area of "do good or do harm." Resolve to do good.

STRATEGY TWELVE

Testing: There Shouldn't Be Anything Standard About It

I said earlier that students with learning challenges are more than their paperwork, and I sincerely believe that. Unfortunately, there will always be cases when the student with learning challenges will be judged primarily by that paperwork. Therefore, it would be exceedingly foolish not to make every effort to have that paperwork present the student accurately and in the best possible light.

There are three basic purposes for testing. First, testing is used for determining diagnosis and assessing eligibility for specific services. Second, testing is used to gain understanding of one's learning style that will enable effective learning and teaching strategies. Third, barrier testing is used to attempt to eliminate potential failure and forecast potential success in a given environment.

School districts often do an excellent job in the first two testing categories, but in my experience, they have less expertise in presenting a student's potential for success. It is a question of focus and interpretation. School districts rarely have reason to focus on strengths and emphasize potentials. For this reason, when updating documentation that will be used by post-secondary admissions (around the student's junior year in high school) you must be very specific about the purpose for which testing will be used and that you want to highlight strengths and potential.

During my junior year in high school, I had to update my Woodcock-Johnson and Wechsler Adult Intelligence Scale examinations for the colleges to which I was applying. I wanted to accentuate the positive and show that I had acquired the skills and possessed the potential to succeed in their programs. I took these tests with a private company. While one is taking the test, the proctor cannot in any way alter the format of the test. However, after different sections of the test are completed, the proctor can "re-present" the material using different accommodations. This is called "accommodated testing" or "limit testing." For example, when I took the Reading Comprehension section of the test that asked me to read and fill in the blanks, I struggled through that section because of my poor reading level and not because of comprehension deficits. Taken normally, I scored at a level consistent with a freshman in high school. When my proctor administered the testing in an oral format, reading the test to me as a reader would with my legal accommodations and leaving me to fill in the blanks, I scored significantly above my grade level. My proctor still scored the tests in the correct standardized way but was also able to write a note in the interpretation of the test to show how my score improved when I was given the proper accommodations. This, in turn, showed that my issue was the reading of the test itself and not with my comprehension of its content. I am sure this was reassuring to the admissions departments at the colleges I applied to and might have tipped the scales toward my acceptances in spite of low testing scores.

Testers in private agencies are dedicated solely to your child's interests and while they will not skew the test results, they can certainly accentuate legitimate skills and strengths and showcase your child's potential. Sometimes it is worth every penny to get a professional private agency to administer the testing during your student's junior or senior year. Just be sure to let them know what use you intend to make of their report.

When testing with a public agency or school, under the law, you have the right to a pre-testing meeting, sometimes referred to as the "evaluation plan" or the "review of existing data." Be sure to take advantage of this meeting. It is your opportunity to understand what the examiners are testing for and why. It is also your opportunity to request that "accommodated testing" as described above be conducted if you desire. You also have the right to request specific tests that might showcase your student's abilities. As a parent, it is difficult to know which tests will be most efficacious. For a small fee, a private testing agency, after reviewing previous testing, can advise which tests would be most effective for your student. You need not hire them to administer the tests. If the public agency or school refuses your requests for specific tests or for "accommodated" testing, you have the right to ask for their reasons in writing. If your requests are reasonable, you will generally find the agency cooperative. However, you should know that, should you choose, you have the option to pursue due process and possibly oblige the school to deliver on your requests or for the school to pay for private testing. By law, the school must inform you of your rights and help you, if needed, to understand them. You might have access to an advocacy group who could also help with this process; ask the school for a way to contact an advocacy agency if the school does not automatically offer this information. MPACT (an agency funded by the U.S. Department of Education) provides advocacy information to Missouri parents. Similar agencies exist in most other states and communities.

Many students with learning challenges score very poorly on the ACT and the SAT. These scores are often not true representations of a student's actual abilities. Fortunately, some fine colleges and universities do not rely exclusively on these examinations in their admissions processes. Others will accept an essay explaining why these tests do not accurately portray a student's abilities. I used this option and attached a letter to my applications stating why my ACT scores did not reflect my potential.

Conversely, if your students are taking lower-level courses in high school, or are spending a lot of time in academic support programs, make sure that they apply only to colleges that are appropriate to their actual abilities. In other words, ensure that your students do not fall into the trap of being accepted to a school that will prove too challenging, thereby setting them up for failure.

Examples of barrier testing are the college admissions departments' use of minimum SAT or ACT and Achievement Test scores as hard and fast barriers. Most students with learning challenges are eligible for special accommodations for all these tests. Everything from extended time, calculators, tests on tape, readers, scribes, and so on, is available if the proper documentation is provided on a timely basis. Students with learning challenges must keep their documentation up to date. Double check on how current it must be for the various college entrance examinations as well as for post-secondary admissions departments. Contact the standardized testing companies and find out the current requirements for providing accommodations. Accommodations can often take several months to set up. Sometimes accommodations are initially denied and additional documentation must be provided to the testing agency to secure what the student legally deserves. Students with learning challenges should take advantage of everything they are due. Try to work out a manageable plan for administering these tests. My high school originally intended to pull me out of classes for five successive mornings in order for me to take the ACT. Not only could I not afford to miss my regular classes, as few students with learning challenges could, but you can imagine how this would have worked out for my concentration on the test itself. As it turned out, I took my ACT on tape during my school district's summer session. It took five hours and a lot of rewinding. My results were not spectacular, but I did not fall behind in my regular courses either. You might find compromises like this beneficial for your students with learning challenges.

Checklist for Strategy Twelve:

- It is important to understand the various assessments given to students and why each is administered.

- Testing is used to determine diagnosis and eligibility, find successful teaching strategies, and is used in barrier testing.

- Public schools are very good at the first two types of tests, but it can be beneficial to have barrier testing done by an outside source.

- Make sure to utilize all accommodations available for barrier tests such as ACT, SAT, and Achievement Tests.

- Be sure that all documentation is up-to-date and submitted in a timely fashion for testing.

- Make sure all accommodations provided for the student are administered in a way that actually benefits the student.

Especially for:

Students

Tests, whether for diagnosis or for measuring academic achievement, are all stressful. They are also necessary if you are to be allowed the special help and accommodations you need in order to learn most effectively. Understand that many tests are designed to show off your strengths and demonstrate your abilities as much as they expose your weaknesses. It is important to always give your best effort on any test or assessment so that the results are a legitimate reflection of your present skills and can be used to help you learn. It is just as important for you to be part of the discussion that explains your test performance in order for you to learn where your strengths and deficits lie. Any good evaluation should include specific strategies for exploiting your learning strengths and suggestions for remediating or compensating for your weaknesses. Make sure you understand these recommendations and exactly how they will help you to learn.

Parents

As always, you are your child's best advocate. In testing it is especially important that you understand why testing is being administered and for what purpose it will be used. Understand the difference between testing to qualify for services for your child and testing that you wish to use to demonstrate skills, accomplishments or potential. Demand appropriate testing for the purpose you intend. When the results are explained to you, make sure that you truly understand the strengths and weaknesses the testing reveals. Be sure that the recommendations for teaching modifications and approaches make sense to you based on the explanation of the test results. Try to include your child in the test explanation process as much as is appropriate so that he or she has the opportunity to understand his or her own learning style, or to "learn how to learn."

<u>Educators</u>

Do identify and consider the purposes for the evaluations that you are administering: diagnostic; to determine eligibility for services or accommodations; illumination of teaching strategies; and/or progress measurement. If the testing is for barrier purposes or for admissions testing, it would be very desirable to present the student in the best possible light. Know that you have the option of administering "accommodated testing" or "limit testing" and commenting on the improved performance when appropriate accommodations are provided. This does take extra time but might make the difference as to whether a student is admitted to a desired post-secondary program, which, in turn, affects the student's future career. The small inconvenience for you can make a very large difference for the student.

Also, when scheduling any testing for a student with learning challenges, be sure to consider attention span, class time missed, fatigue and other issues that might affect the student's performance both on the test and other course work.

Try to include the student in at least part of the test interpretation. It is important for the student as well as his or her parents to understand the strengths and weaknesses that the testing reveals. Try to make results and recommendations for learning strategies as concrete and understandable as possible to both parents and the student.

Remember always how extremely emotional it is for both parents and students to hear test results. Stressing strengths and progress over weaknesses and deficits and presenting alternative modes and strategies for learning can remove some of the sting from disappointing results. Kindness and tact are almost as important as accuracy and clarity. A gentle reminder to parents and students that test results represent only a snapshot in time and that improvements are possible and worth striving for are kind concepts to include in your evaluation discussions.

STRATEGY THIRTEEN
Use All the Resources Available

ACCOMMODATIONS

Encourage your students to use all the resources available to them. Many students with learning challenges are reluctant to use some accommodations for which they qualify because they are embarrassed or because arranging for them seems like too much trouble. Teachers and parents should assure their students that it is their right to receive accommodations and encourage their students to recognize that it is their responsibility to utilize all accommodations in order to achieve their full potential.

Tutors

Tutors are not new technology, but they are a type of resource that can put success within reach of the student with learning challenges. Tutors do not do course work for the student, but they can re-teach, drill and proofread. Free or paid, if a student with learning challenges needs tutors to succeed, help him or her find the appropriate help. Many schools will provide professional or peer tutors either free or for very reasonable fees. Mentoring programs like Big Brothers and Big Sisters might also be able to match students up with retired special education teachers. Churches, synagogues and public libraries are possible resources. Parents often try to fill this need. I think it is a mistake. Parents are not professional tutors and parental tutoring can add significantly to the stress of the parent-child relationship. Students also benefit from becoming adept at working with a variety of professionals. It might be easier for students to get a parent to read material to them than to scan it into a computer or listen to it on tape, but students will end up paying for this bad habit their first semester away at college. I hate to admit it, but without tutors to re-teach, drill and proofread, I would have been up a creek.

Readers

A reader for exams is crucial to the success of many a student with learning challenges. I can read, but decoding is still a difficult process. I often lose the exact meaning of a question. By reading along with a reader (or a tape), I can be sure of clearly understanding what a teacher's exam questions are asking. For students with attention problems, a reader keeps the student focused. Some students who can read aloud perfectly cannot comprehend what they are reading, but when the same passage is read to them they can comprehend perfectly. They are auditory rather than visual learners. Readers can help a broad variety of learning styles that different students present.

Scribes

A scribe allows the student to dictate exam answers and writes verbatim what the student dictates. Many students with learning challenges have difficulty getting their thoughts on paper. The physical act of writing distracts them and they lose their train of thought. A scribe can alleviate this problem. Sometimes the physical act of writing has been so challenging for a student that he/she has totally given up on tasks involving the requirement to express knowledge and ideas in written form. Don't let this happen; a scribe can help assume the physical part of writing so that the important part, the ideas the student has, can be demonstrated to others.

Peer note-takers

In some courses, the process of writing and spelling is so time and energy-consuming that the student with learning challenges cannot observe what the professor is demonstrating on the board or pay close enough attention to understand the content of the lecture and take useful notes at the same time. Peer note-takers are students in the same course assigned by the teacher or disability support services to provide a copy of their class notes to the student with learning challenges. Peer notes free one up to concentrate fully on what is being presented in class. Remember, note-takers are in addition to class attendance, not a substitute for it.

Basic computers

We all know how valuable word processors and spell check have been to students with learning challenges. All students with learning challenges need computers of their own. Computers are affordable enough now for nearly everyone to be able to have one. For less than $500 a student can have a computer, printer, software and internet access. Encourage students' families to get a basic computer and to arrange whatever training the student needs to use it effectively. The training is essential. A computer program you cannot operate only adds to frustration.

Extended time and quiet testing areas

Both of these accommodations are critically beneficial to most students with learning challenges and especially those with distractibility and attention issues. They have to be scheduled, but are worth the extra effort. Be careful, though, that extended time doesn't mean getting behind because so much time is needed to complete tasks; sometimes extended time can be coupled with assignment reductions. Also, many students might need to have that extended time distributed into segments, which some refer to as "blocks of time;" working on a test for four straight hours might be counterproductive for many students.

Audio Books

Books on CD or audio files are not new either, but the market has shifted from serving only the visually impaired to including audio for students with learning challenges as well. The trend is moving towards more books for school and college-age users and more emphasis on textbook recording. Now some publishers are making their texts available for download directly to a computer. After download, a screen reader program can read the text aloud. Now, as a college instructor, the textbook publishers provide this type of download to me and I use it for all my texts.

Audio texts are crucial to students like me who have severe reading problems. Students who manage the reading load in high school might find that college reading demands are beyond them. I often had 300 to 500 pages to read each night as an undergraduate student.

Even when students with learning challenges are still in the process of reading remediation, tapes can be extremely beneficial. Even if students use audio recordings primarily for pleasure reading, that will provide them with exposure to more material—and we all know what that does for vocabularies and VFOGIs—vast funds of general information. Also, reading along with audio has shown to improve reading skills for some students. Tapes are a great way for slow readers to keep up with what their peers are reading and a painless way to work through the more arcane classics.

Help students with learning challenges find all the audio sources available. There are many, but do not assume that all texts are already available in audio form. My experience in college is that only about one-third of the material is available on audio. Believe me, I panicked in December when I registered for January courses knowing that I would not have half of the texts that I needed by the beginning of classes.

The major source, Learning Ally (formally called Recordings for the Blind and Dyslexic) can have a two-year lead time to produce material upon request. Any audio-dependent student will need to find additional and more responsive sources. Some reading pads like Kindle and Nook pads can read aloud from e-book files. Some cannot. Research products carefully before buying.

I could not have succeeded in college without St. Louis Talking Tapes, and I am sure that their volunteer readers were happier than even my parents were when I graduated.

Audio Books /CD/Download Sources

Learning Ally (formally called Recordings for the Blind and Dyslexic), Princeton, NJ 1-800-221-4792. Learning Ally has the largest library of audio textbooks for all ages, and is a not-for-profit organization.

www.learningally.org

BookShare

www.bookshare.org

Similar to Learning Ally, but not free.

Books-on-Tape, Newport Beach, CA 1-800-252-6996. For-profit, Books-on-Tape is a large library of classic fiction and nonfiction available for a rental fee.

www.booksontape.com

Blackstone Audio books, Ashland, OR 1-800-729-2665. For-profit, Blackstone Audio is a large library of classic fiction and nonfiction available for a rental fee.

www.blackstoneaudio.com

Wolfner Library for the Blind and Physically Handicapped, Jefferson City, MO tape library, is free to handicapped residents of Missouri.

www.sos.mo.gov/wolfner/

Note: Most states have a service similar to Wolfner. Contact your local library.

Checklist for Strategy Thirteen:

- Be sure to utilize all legal accommodations that students are entitled to.

Especially For:

Students

Use it all. Accommodations are your equalizers. Don't allow shyness or embarrassment to limit your use of accommodations. You would not expect a classmate who needs glasses to see the blackboard to be required to leave his or her glasses at home just because all students do not have the advantage of having glasses. Your accommodations are fair for you and you deserve them. Accommodations can save time and effort and used right they can put academic success within your reach.

Parents

Encourage your children to take advantage of all the accommodations they have a legal right to receive. Try to seek out good mentors and tutors and make them your child's cheerleaders.

Educators

For your students with learning challenges, develop their competence and independence in their use of accommodations. Help them to learn what they need, how to obtain accommodations they need, as well as how to use them. Also, help other students to understand that accommodations are "fair" and do not give learning challenged students any more of an advantage than eyeglasses or hearing aids.

ADAPTIVE

TECHNOLOGIES

STRATEGY FOURTEEN

The Magic of Technology

Adaptive technology, which I will focus on in this section, is just another, more modern form of accommodation. Yesterday it was magic, today it is amazing and tomorrow it will be standard.

I will try to give you an overview of current adaptive technology for students with learning challenges: What it can do and what it *cannot* do; where to get it; and how to use it both inside and outside the classroom. I am not a technological wizard. However, in the past, as a student, and now as a college instructor with my own learning challenges, I have used a variety of adaptive devices and programs over the last three decades.

The new technological advances are truly exciting for those of us with learning challenges. I hope that when you finish this section you will have a new view of what these new technologies can do for you or your students.

Technology is one trend that is moving in the student's favor. I believe it is going to be the equalizer for students with learning challenges. Much of its early product was developed for the benefit of the blind. Now researchers and manufacturers are recognizing the enormity of the learning challenges market and are developing products tailor-made for this population. This shift, and the trend of newer e-readers, mp3 books and apps, will make it much easier for students with learning challenges to use the products, and the size of the market will ensure continued research and development of new and better products.

I started using a program called OpenBook about 20+ years ago. It allowed me to scan a book into my computer, and the program read it aloud to me with about 75% accuracy. Magic! But it was DOS-based and I had to learn all kinds of obscure commands to get it to work. It might have been easier just to learn to read! OpenBook used the same voice as Stephen Hawking's speech program, and for years I had the sense that Stephen was my personal tutor. I am using the same product today, and after about 10 upgrades, it is terrifically user-friendly. There is a choice of voices now, but I still have Stephen.

Today, I can scan a printed book or handout into my computer and it will read it back to me aloud with nearly perfect accuracy. I can even edit the scanned text on my word processor and print it out.

I can dictate text into my voice recognition program and the words I say appear on my computer screen, ready to be edited, spell checked, grammar checked and printed. And then it is read back to me aloud.

I can log onto the Internet and my screen reader will read my emails aloud to me. Additionally, I can dictate email messages to my friends. I can even spell check them—*a very good thing!*

My screen reader can read aloud any text I find on the Internet for research, and I can cut and paste that text into a word processor to edit and print.

There is a hand held scanning device that will read aloud as it passes over a line of print. This is useful if you are away from a computer or want to read your phone bill.

Voice In Voice Out is introducing a service that will be completely voice interactive over the computer microphone or telephone. This will be useful for all kinds of daily life tasks such as making airline reservations or purchases online.

I believe that in the near future all newly printed books, newspapers and magazines will be available in digital form, which will enable them to be read aloud by computer voice. Think about what that will mean to students who now wait months for a textbook in order for it to be recorded by a volunteer!

So what is out there today that your students can use and afford? All of the above, plus.

Franklin Spellers

These have been around for a long time. They are used to read aloud any word typed in, as well as to give choices for misspelled words. There are still a few that pronounce the word aloud. They are mobile and very handy.

Scanners and Optical Character Recognition (OCR) Programs

A $99 scanner allows me to scan printed pages onto my computer screen. There are several programs that will read those scanned pages aloud back to me. A scanner is invaluable for materials not available in audio such as last-minute handouts, study guides and library materials. I have used an OCR program called "OpenBook" since tenth grade. It is a life saver when tapes do not show up in time or professors assign last-minute library reading assignments. It is important to understand the limitations of scanners. They cannot scan script and they cannot scan poorly printed documents. Students with learning challenges who use scanners must educate their teachers so they realize that the quality of printing matters. Some professors still don't get it! And that is why tutors and readers are not obsolete yet.

Hand Scanners

Hand scanners are a relatively new device that reads aloud when you run them over a line of text. They are independent of a computer, and therefore mobile. Quicktionary Reading Pen II is an example of this technology.

Speech Recognition Software

Several programs will allow you to dictate your ideas into the computer's microphone. The program will convert your speech instantly, and it will print it on the computer's screen in order for it to be edited and printed. For the student with weak spelling or writing skills, this program can release tremendous pent-up creativity.

I have used Dragon Dictate for several years, and other manufacturers are bringing new programs on the market almost daily. Dragon's newer products are really very good. The program still has to be "trained" to recognize your voice, but the training time has decreased dramatically over the years.

It will hold voice files for multiple users and therefore can be used in a school setting quite economically. It does, however, require a quiet room, because background noise affects its accuracy.

Screen Readers

These programs will read aloud anything I can get onto my computer screen. They will read anything from CD-ROM encyclopedias to thesauri and dictionaries. They will read aloud anything I access from the Internet. They read my emails aloud to me. For weak readers or auditory learners, this is a godsend. Products included in this list are: NaturalReader, TextAloud, Read Please, EReader (Cast), JAWS (Freedom Scientific), and Kurzweil 3000. These programs are not affected by background noise, but their voices do drive others to distraction. One can use earphones, but students with learning challenges truly need a dorm or study room to themselves. Roommates would kill them after the first week! College Special Needs departments seem to understand about these needs, and they can influence housing assignments in favor of the student with learning challenges.

Word Anticipation Programs

These software programs are designed for poor spellers or aphasics. They use context and initial letters to suggest appropriate words. I have a friend who is also a stroke victim, and he uses Co-Writer and raves about it. There is also one called SoothSayer Word Prediction.

Every day there is much more wonderful technology and there will be much more to come. Make a point of keeping up with new advances. Attending LD conferences such as LDA, or other special-needs organizations, surfing the Internet, and contacting disability support services at local colleges are excellent resources for keeping up with adaptive technology.

LIST OF ADAPTIVE TECHNOLOGY SOURCES

Franklin Spellers

www.franklin.com

Scanners and OCR Programs
OpenBook (LD friendly)

www.freedomscientific.com

SARA (all in one kit)

www.freedomscientific.com

Kurzweil 1000TM (Blind/Low Vision Group)

www.kurzweiledu.com

Hand Scanners
The Quicktionary Reading Pen

Reading Pens and Dictionaries

www.quick-pen.com

www.innovationhouse.com

Speech Recognition Software
Dragon Naturally Speaking

www.nuance.com

Screen Readers

NaturalReader

A good free software.

www.naturalreaders.com

TextAloud

For Windows PC that converts your text from MS Word Documents, Web Pages, Emails and PDF Files into natural-sounding speech.

www.nextup.com

Read Please

A good free software.

www.readplease.com

EReader (Cast)

www.cast.org

JAWS (Freedom Scientific) (Blind/Low Vision Group)

www.freedomscientific.com

Kurzweil 3000

www.kurzweiledu.com

Word Anticipation Programs

Co-Writer

www.donjohnston.com

SoothSayer Word Prediction

www.ahf-net.com

The Internet

It is almost as if the Internet was designed for students with learning challenges. The search engines make research possible for non-readers who cannot make much use of anything they might be lucky enough to unearth in a traditional library. The amount of accessible information is beyond comprehension.

Finding information requires specialized, but easily learned skills. Parents or educators, encourage your students to get in-depth, one-on-one, hands-on instruction in Internet searching. It will be the skill of the future and one of the most empowering gifts you can give them.

Technology is one trend that is moving in a direction that will favor the student with learning challenges. It is going to be the equalizer for students with learning challenges. Encourage your students and their parents to find out about these programs and to keep informed about new technology. Better yet, find out about them yourself and become a technology advisor to your students. I use them all, and they literally made college possible for me.

Coordinating It All

Scanners, screen readers, word-processing programs and voice recognition programs all have to work compatibly together. While this requires less of a technological miracle *today* than it did ten years ago, I would recommend getting clear advice on what works with what before you go out and buy a bunch of separate components. You can count on the fact that your old word-processing program will not like your new dictation program, and that the first scanner you buy will ignore your OCR program. A few years ago, I bought a new scanner, having been told by my OCR program people that any of three would be compatible. Naturally, the one I chose did not work with it and it had to be exchanged. Screen Reader or Voice Recognition program dealers usually can help a lot. They can recommend which other components work best with their program. Be sure that they understand all the functions that are important to you and that they are able and willing to stick around until the whole package works together. The disabilities support department at your local college or junior college might be helpful for advice on what they are using and for recommending who is a committed dealer in your area. At the high-school level, the special education teacher and/or the school IT teacher should be able to assist you.

Training

Training on how to use these programs and how to make them work together is essential. You do not have to be learning challenged to become confused. My first adaptive products were designed for the blind and my first computer advisor was blind himself. The programs were DOS-based and had hundreds of commands that I did not need and that only confused me. He could not differentiate between what I needed and what I did not need. We made it work eventually, but it was quite a painful introduction to technology!

Voice recognition programs must "train" to your voice. The dealers who sell them will provide some training. I suggest finding someone else willing to devote the time to teaching you and your student how to use these tools. Again, the special education teacher at your high school or the disability support department of your local college or junior college might be good contact points. It is super-critical that all these programs work together and that your student is very familiar with using them all well before beginning a post-secondary program away from home. Technical glitches and a steep learning curve are impossible over long-distance calls and when you do not have the same programs on your computers. The IT people at your student's college might not be familiar with these programs either.

Space

A computer, monitor, printer, scanner, microphone, speakers, etc. all take up considerable space. My first dorm room needed an additional desk and that left me about three square feet of floor space. I had to crawl over the bed to get to the desk. Be sure to buy a lot of power strips. There are literally dozens of plugs and wires. I am surprised that the whole dorm did not power down when I turned my system on. I am sure that if Bates College knew how much power I pulled, they would have raised their tuition rate for me!

Using this new technology has a learning curve of its own. It takes research to find the programs that are right for your needs. It takes training to use them effectively. It takes real self-discipline and support to stick with them in the beginning. It is much easier to get your mother to read material than to scan it or to listen to it yourself on audio. But dedicated practice will bring independence. And using new technology is getting more user-friendly and affordable every day.

I hope I did not make these technological packages seem too daunting to put together. They really are not, and the benefits they provide far outweigh the effort of learning about them. Adaptive technology has contributed immensely to making my academic dreams come true. I hope that this information will be helpful in your quest.

But there is more to successful use of accommodations and adaptive technology than just hardware and software. It takes an attitude of belief in your possibilities from you and from your parents and educators. It takes continuous advocacy for yourself and by yourself. It takes the help and support of countless others along the way.

Checklist for Strategy Fourteen:

- Be sure to utilize ALL sources of help for your student, both traditional and high-tech.

- Training, space, and coordination are all important in the use of adaptive technologies.

- Disability support departments in local colleges and junior colleges can be invaluable resources in coordinating adaptive technologies. Special education teachers will be a support at the high-school level.

- Be sure part of a student's IEP includes assistive technology needs.

Especially For:

Students

Adaptive technologies are magical equalizers. They might require some training time until you can take full advantage of them, but it is well worth your time. The best and the brightest are working overtime to create new programs and applications just for you. Try to keep up with the newest advancements.

Parents

Encourage your children to take advantage of all the accommodations they have a legal right to receive. Try to make adaptive technology available to them and learn how to use it yourself so that you can coach and encourage your child to make the most of it. At the high-school level, ask for an assistive technology evaluation if needed, and/or make sure technology needs are included in your student's IEP.

Educators

Become an adaptive-technology maven so you can introduce your students and their parents to its magic. Lobby for installation and use of adaptive technology in the resource-room and classrooms of your school. Make your students competent and independent in their use of both accommodations and adaptive technology.

Conclusion

The most critical message I wish to share with you in writing this book is to always believe in possibilities—possibilities for yourself as a student with learning challenges; possibilities as the parent of a student with learning challenges; and as an educator, possibilities for your students who are coping with learning challenges. Learning challenges are real challenges and they take bravery, creativity and hope to overcome. If you believe that anything is possible and that miracles can be made to happen, you are well on your way to turning your dreams into realities.

Your journey will be uniquely yours and likely quite different from mine. I have suggested many strategies and cautions for students, and their parents and educators, in these pages. These strategies have worked well for me and I sincerely hope many of them prove useful to you and make your path to your goals a bit easier.

One final caution for students which applies to all young people, not just those with learning challenges: try to make sure that your dreams and goals are truly yours and are what you believe you want for yourself. It is very easy to get caught up in the process, or to become committed to living up to your parents' or mentors' expectations for you. Also, others might put down your dreams and discourage you from trying to achieve what you want to achieve. This is primarily your journey. Stop occasionally to reassess the path you are treading so that it leads you to where you truly want to be.

Always take the time to celebrate your successes both large and small. Your successes will be the result of extra effort and careful planning. They are accomplishments worthy of real celebration.

Finally, there is no way to make this journey on your own. Those who love, respect, advocate and go the extra mile to put your dreams within your reach deserve your admiration. Remember always to honor those who have helped you along your way. It is as a team that you and your mentors make the miracles happen and the dreams come true. Don't ever feel that you should have to accomplish a task without help or support from others in order to take ownership of what you do. Almost everyone, not only those with extra learning needs, connects with others to achieve maximum success. In fact, by recognizing which supports you need and asking for them, you are adding another accomplishment to your list of which you should feel proud.

So, students, remember to accept yourself, believe in yourself, and advocate for yourself.

Parents, remember to accept your child with all of his or her strengths and challenges, believe in possibilities for your child, and advocate for all of the educational services and programs your child requires in order to achieve success.

Educators, please accept your students including all of their learning challenges, believe your students are capable of achieving success, and provide support to accommodate their learning needs while teaching them to become independent learners.

A Guide for Getting into the

Right

Post-Secondary Program

You Can't Start Too Soon

If there is one thing that I have emphasized throughout this book, it is that preparation is the key to success for the student with learning challenges. You really cannot start too early with post-secondary planning. Visiting schools on a family trip during your freshman or sophomore year is not a bad idea. I understand you might not be fully aware of your student's full capabilities or interests by their freshman or sophomore years, and therefore cannot be assured which programs are going to be the best fit, but, these visits are vital to condition a student to the interview process and to the post-secondary environment.

Developing a post-secondary résumé starts years before visits to actual programs. It starts with course choices all through high school. Basic courses or Advanced Placement courses? Choose the most challenging program your student can succeed in without burnout. Sometimes academic advisors of learning challenged students are hesitant to recommend more demanding options and parents and the student might have to advocate for the choices they think are best.

Summers and weekends are opportunities for volunteer activities or extracurricular courses, both of which are valuable experiences and look good on résumés. I volunteered at a variety of day and sleepover camps for disadvantaged or handicapped children, and one summer I took a statistics course at a local community college. The purpose of the statistics course was to get a head start on a course I knew would be required for my major and could be very difficult for me. If I did badly in the community college course, I would not have to include it in my résumé, but if I did well it would demonstrate my ability to succeed at the college level, a no-lose bet.

School extracurricular activities and competitive sports should be chosen carefully. Make sure that the time commitment is balanced against the benefit.

Overall, your goal is to create a history of activities that present a well-rounded, responsible, motivated, and academically competent student who is coping successfully with his or her learning challenges. A convincing résumé like this takes years to assemble.

Letters of Recommendation from Teachers

This is the time to utilize those teacher questionnaires from Strategy Ten which you have been collecting throughout the student's high-school experience. It is very important to identify two or three teachers who might want to write a letter of recommendation for pertinent post-secondary programs. Go through the questionnaires and find the teachers who had very positive things to say. You can also offer to the teacher a copy of the completed questionnaire as a memory refresher if the student is not presently in one of the teacher's classes. The student should ask if the teacher is comfortable writing a positive recommendation letter—even if the previous evaluation was positive. It is not only a courtesy, but you want positive and enthusiastic letters. Depending on the student's academic strengths and weaknesses, it might be beneficial to inform the teacher about all of the support services and accommodations the post-secondary program will be providing if the student is accepted. Knowing that the proper support services will be in place, the teacher might feel more comfortable about the student's chances for success and thereby, can write a more enthusiastic recommendation letter.

The Student & Parents Must Take the Lead Role

Most likely, if a student is in a public school or in a private school not specifically geared to learning challenged education, it will be up to the parent and the student to take the lead in looking for post-secondary programs that are going to be the best fit for you. The reason for this is that many advisors simply are not familiar with the requirements that a student with learning challenges will have. It is doubtful that they will be familiar with the amazingly broad range of support services offered by many different programs, much less have any knowledge of the specialized admissions processes many of these programs have. Special education teachers might be familiar with some programs, but their knowledge is not usually extensive; this is not their main area of expertise. It is very important for the parent and student to be part of this search and decision. Even if you hire a consultant, it is important for you to be a major part of the process. Parents, no one knows your child better than you do, and students, no professional knows you better than you know yourself.

During the spring of my junior year in high school, my parents and I met with my college advisor who unfortunately had no experience with colleges with learning challenges services. That meant that all the responsibility for research into colleges fell upon my mother. This is not unusual even in excellent private and public schools, and sometimes even at schools that specialize in special needs.

Knowledge of learning-support systems in post-secondary programs is very specialized and limited. My mother and I pored over college guides and came up with a list of appropriate programs which seemed to have adequate support services. My college advisor suggested Bates College as a school that met my chosen criteria, with the important exception that Bates lacked strong support. Bates, he said, was very competitive and would be a stretch for me. No one from my high school had ever been accepted by Bates. I was immediately intrigued. When my mother and I researched Bates, I immediately liked it despite the fact that it broke all the rules for my mother's school investigation system and thus ignored all her hard work! By the fall of senior year, we had visited more than 20 schools, and I had fallen in love with Bates, naturally! I decided to apply for "early decision" there, hoping to increase my chance of acceptance.

I got my early decision acceptance from Bates College, December 15, 1995. I was totally psyched. I really began to feel that all my hard work and dedication had finally started to pay off and my dreams had started to come true.

Research LD Programs

There are several good books out there on different types and levels of learning challenge support programs. Some examples are: *The K&W Guide to Colleges for Students with Learning Disabilities or Attention Deficit/Hyperactivity Disorder* (2010), *Colleges for Students with Learning Disabilities or AD/HD* (2007), and *Peterson's Two-Year Colleges* (2011). These catalogues categorize colleges and universities into three categories or levels of disability support services. The three categories are 1) Structured Programs ("SP"), 2) Coordinated Services ("CS") and 3) Services ("S"). "Structured Programs" are defined as those programs that go beyond mandated services and "might include special admissions procedures, specialized and trained professionals, compensatory strategies, one-on-one tutoring, additional fees, compulsory participation, and monitoring" (Kravets & Wax, p. 3). "Coordinated Services" are "schools that have some involvement with admissions decisions, voluntary participation, more than just mandated services, small or no fees, and less structure" (Kravets & Wax, p. 3). Basic services are services that "comply with Section 504 mandates that rarely have specialized LD staff, do not have monitoring, and are totally dependent on student advocacy" (Kravets & Wax, p. 3).

As I mentioned earlier, I chose a college that had no organized LD support services. They were quite willing to work with me and had one secretary who coordinated readers and scribes and note-takers. She tried to provide peer tutors, but that did not work, because the tutors often failed to show up for appointments. I provided my own tutors and I chose to arrange for my own books-on-tape a good deal of the time. Because I had learned about and used these systems in high school, I was well prepared to obtain them for myself in college. Still, it was an added expense, but I graduated with good grades. On the other hand, the university I chose for graduate school had a more extensive support department which could provide books-on-tape and screen-reading programs, as well as other services from which I benefited. They also had a special learning challenge support program called The Achieve Program for an additional fee; this program provided tutors, organizational skills classes, mentoring, and extensive supervision so that students with learning challenges did not get lost in the cracks. Your student's academic strengths and weaknesses, organizational skills and level of motivation should guide your selection of appropriate support programs.

Post-Secondary Questionnaires

Post-Secondary Questionnaires are additional aids that parents and students can use when visiting and evaluating post-secondary programs. The college guides mentioned above and individual program brochures are all useful; however, their data is from the post-secondary programs' own brochures and might have changed since the brochure or guide was printed. It is very important to know if there is other information about the program that you should know. For example, take the scenario where a college seems like a really good program, but the program has lost funding since its brochure was produced. As a result of this, the school now has a staff of three serving 300 students with learning challenges instead of a ratio of 1-to-30 which the brochure states. It is important for you to know this. The staff might be wonderful, but with this ratio, they cannot serve the needs of the students. It will be useful to ask these questions first of the learning challenges support program staff and then to a student peer who uses these services. Feel free to add any questions to the questionnaire below that are particular to your student's needs.

A few years ago as part of my master's thesis and while working at the transitions department of a high school for students with learning challenges, I visited 20 or more schools offering a variety of post-secondary support programs. My experience in visiting and interviewing the staffs of these programs at all three support levels showed that the actual services that the staffs were providing differed greatly from the services their brochures advertised. It was almost as if the staffs had never read their own brochures! Some of these programs were doing an excellent job and the students were successful and satisfied. Some that looked good on paper were simply not meeting students' needs with services as promised. The point is that you really have to check it out. For example, if it is important for your student to have the foreign-language requirement waived to graduate, make sure that that is present policy and get it in writing when your child is accepted. A good friend of mine attended a college that initially promised him foreign-language deferment and during his junior year the college changed their policy. It was a real hassle getting his diploma and degree from them. If your student must have someone to review his or her assignment book every day, confirm that the program can provide this service. Interviewing on the phone is fine for confirming ratios and specific services, but only a visit can show the character of the staff, students and campus. It is really the only way to interact with students presently utilizing the program.

Interview Questions for
School/College/University Staff

Program: _____

Date Completed: _____

General Questions about the Learning Disability Support Program or to be modified for your applicable learning, social or physical challenge.

Is there a LD Program?	Yes/No
Is there a specific person in charge of the LD program?	Yes/No
If so, what are his/her qualifications?	
How long has the program been in existence?	
Is there a central place where students can go to access help?	Yes/No
Is diagnostic testing required for admission to program?	Yes/No
If so, is it done by program personnel?	Yes/No

What is the cost?	$
Is the ACT required?	Yes/No
What is the minimum score for admission?	
Is the SAT required?	Yes/No
What is the minimum score for admission?	
Are there other admissions requirements for the LD program?	Yes/No
If so, what are they?	
Are waivers granted for classes which are impacted by the learning disability? (Example: Foreign language waiver?)	Yes/No
Is there a new student orientation for the LD program?	Yes/No
Is there any kind of priority registration or assistance in class registration for students in the LD program?	Yes/No
Are remedial/developmental courses required?	Yes/No
Are any other college preparatory classes offered?	Yes/No
Is a foreign language required?	Yes/No

Is there a foreign language waiver?	Yes/No
Is there a flow chart that indicates which staff is responsible for which services?	Yes/No

Tutors:

Are tutors provided?	Yes/No
Are tutors assigned by subject area?	Yes/No
Are the procedures for requesting/obtaining tutors clearly defined?	Yes/No
Is there an extra cost for tutors?	Yes/No
Is so, what is it?	$
Is there a tutor supervisor?	Yes/No
What kind of training do tutors receive?	
Professional or peer tutors?	
Who makes the arrangements for meeting with tutor(s)?	
Where do you meet with your tutor(s)?	

Course Accommodations:

Un-timed tests	Yes/No
Note-takers	Yes/No
Extended time	Yes/No

Computers	Yes/No
Readers: for assignments	Yes/No
Use of tape recorders in lecture	Yes/No
Copies of class notes	Yes/No
Audio Books /CD	Yes/No
Proof readers	Yes/No
Calculators for tests	Yes/No

Library:

Assistance or training for use of library?	Yes/No

Computers:

Is there a computer lab?	Yes/No
Is help available?	Yes/No
How many computers are available?	#
Are printers available?	Yes/No
Are scanners available?	Yes/No
Other computer equipment?	
Are laptop computers allowed in classes for note-taking?	Yes/No

Student Advocacy:

Is there a person to act as a mediator between student and faculty?	Yes/No
How often do advisors meet with students?	
Are there written procedures for advocating?	Yes/No
Is there opportunity for students to self-advocate?	Yes/No

Counseling Services:

Career Planning?	Yes/No
Job coaching/training?	Yes/No
Individual counseling?	Yes/No
LD support group?	Yes/No
Problem solving assistance?	Yes/No
Transition planning?	Yes/No

General Program Questions:

What is the average student/teacher ratio in the classroom?	
What percentage of graduates have jobs waiting when they graduate?	%

What percentage of graduates have learning disabilities?	%

Transportation:

Is there a shuttle service?	Yes/No
Is there public transportation?	Yes/No
If so, is it on campus?	Yes/No

Money:

Do students manage their own money?	Yes/No

(Brehm Preparatory School, 2005)

Does this program have additional LD support beyond what is required by law?	Yes/No
Is there an additional cost over tuition for the LD support program?	Yes/No
If so, what is the cost?	$
How many students are currently being served by the program?	#
Is there a maximum number of hours per week of services a student can use?	Yes/No
What is the ratio of LD support staff to students with LD?	

How many full-time staff members work in the support program?	
Part time?	
Are there LD specialists available?	Yes/No
Are students allowed to take fewer classes and still maintain their full-time status?	Yes/No
Are tutors professional tutors or peer tutors?	Professional/Peer
Will teachers restructure their tests to accommodate the needs of students with LD?	Yes/No
Is there a computer reading machine available?	Yes/No
Is computer dictation software available?	Yes/No
What do you perceive as the weaknesses of the program?	
What are your overall feelings about the program?	
(Phelps, 2000)	

Are there any concerns for the support program's future?	Yes/No
Has the support program been evaluated in the past?	Yes/No
By whom?	
Is the evaluation summary available for students/families?	Yes/No
(ERIC Clearinghouse, 1989)	

Interview Questions for Students

Program: _____

Date Completed: _____

General Questions about the Learning Disability Support Program or to be modified for your applicable learning, social or physical challenge.

Is there an LD Program?	Yes/No
Is there a specific person in charge of the LD program?	Yes/No
Is there a central place where students can go to access help?	Yes/No
Is diagnostic testing required for admission to the program?	Yes/No
If so, is it done by program personnel?	Yes/No
What other admissions requirements did you have to meet?	
Are waivers granted for classes which are affected by the learning disability?	Yes/No

Was there a new student orientation for the LD program?	Yes/No
Is there any kind of priority registration or assistance in registration for students in the LD program?	Yes/No
Are remedial/developmental courses required?	Yes/No
Are any other college preparatory classes offered?	Yes/No
Is a foreign language required?	Yes/No
Is there a flow chart that indicates which staff is responsible for which services?	Yes/No

Tutors:

Are tutors provided?	Yes/No
Are tutors assigned by subject area?	Yes/No
Are the procedures for requesting/obtaining tutors clearly defined?	Yes/No
Who makes the arrangements for meeting with tutor(s)?	
Where does a student meet with a tutor(s)?	

Course Accommodations:	
Un-timed tests	Yes/No
Note-takers	Yes/No
Extended time for assignments/tests by request	Yes/No
Computers	Yes/No
Readers: for assignments	Yes/No
Use of tape recorders in lecture	Yes/No
Copies of class notes	Yes/No
Audio Books /CD	Yes/No
Proofreaders	Yes/No
Calculators for tests	Yes/No

Library:	
Assistance or training for use of library?	Yes/No

Computers:	
Is there a computer lab?	Yes/No
Is help available?	Yes/No
How many computers are available?	#
What kind of computers?	
Are printers available?	Yes/No
Are scanners available?	Yes/No

Other computer equipment?	
What assistive technology is available?	

Student Advocacy:

Is there a person to act as a mediator between student and faculty?	Yes/No
How often do advisors meet with students?	
Are there written procedures for advocating?	Yes/No
Is there opportunity for students to self-advocate?	Yes/No

Counseling Services:

Career Planning?	Yes/No
Job coaching/training?	Yes/No
Individual counseling?	Yes/No
Learning Disability support group?	Yes/No
Problem solving assistance?	Yes/No
Transition planning?	Yes/No

Transportation:

Is there a shuttle service?	Yes/No
Is there public transportation?	Yes/No
If so, is it on campus or near?	Yes/No

Money:

Do students manage their own money?	Yes/No

(Brehm Preparatory School, 2005)

Is there a maximum number of hours per week of support services a student can use?	Yes/No
What is the ratio of LD support staff to students with LD?	
How many full-time staff members work in the support program?	
Part time?	
Are there LD specialists available?	Yes/No
Are students allowed to take fewer classes and still maintain their full-time status?	Yes/No
Are tutors professional tutors or peer tutors? Both?	Professional/ Peer/Both
Will teachers restructure their tests to accommodate the needs of students with LD?	Yes/No

Is there a computer reading machine available?	Yes/No
Is computer dictation software available?	Yes/No
What do you perceive as the strengths of the Learning Disability program?	
What do you perceive as the weaknesses /challenges of the program?	
What are your overall feelings about the program?	
Do you feel that there are enough staff members to accommodate your needs?	Yes/No
Do you feel welcome when you go to discuss or request services?	Yes/No
Does the staff know who you are when you go in?	Yes/No
Is the staff friendly?	Yes/No

Is it simple to request accommodations?	Yes/No
Describe the process you must go through to request accommodations:	
Have you spoken with an LD specialist through the program?	Yes/No
Is it easy to get a tutor?	Yes/No
Is it easy to find/obtain a new tutor if you feel you do not work well with your current tutor?	Yes/No
What do you think the attitude of faculty is toward cooperating with your accommodations?	
What are your class sizes?	
Are you aware of any discrimination from other students because of your LD?	Yes/No
If yes, please comment:	
(Phelps, 2000)	

Learning Challenges Documentation, Testing and Accommodations

Post-secondary accommodations for students with learning challenges are dependent upon their documentation and testing. Be sure to study and follow the specific guidelines for each post-secondary program.

Standardized Testing

Yes, your student will most likely have to take the ACT or SAT. However, many schools are not weighing these tests as heavily as before. There are now websites that list schools that do not require these tests (www.fairtest.org/optstate.html). Be sure your students get all the accommodations that they need and for which they are eligible when they take these tests. Be prepared to fill out forms and to submit current documentation at least a few months before the exam date to get official approval for these accommodations. Take these tests seriously, but, parents and students, do not over-stress yourselves if test results are disappointing. Many schools will let students submit letters stating why they believe the tests do not represent their true abilities. A strong high-school academic record and strong recommendations should go far to mitigate poor ACT or SAT scores.

Start Saving Money

Start saving your coins early and often! College is not cheap! Unfortunately, few students with learning challenges will get honor scholarships. The majority of students with learning challenges will not qualify for Merit Scholarships either. If students take fewer than 12 credit hours per semester, they might not qualify for financial aid. Many students with learning challenges must take lighter course loads in order not to become academically overwhelmed. Be sure to investigate each program's financial aid requirements. It is very important to have the family financially on board for a student's success. Many students with scholarships are required to work on-campus jobs to qualify for financial aid. Students with learning challenges often cannot manage this because of its extra time burden. Many learning challenges support programs, especially those that provide extensive services, charge an additional fee. That fee might be significant. Ask questions in this regard. For any student, college is a big step. This is especially true for a student with learning challenges. Parents should try not to pressure a child into too many extracurricular activities or into a job, and students should try not to over-extend themselves.

Remember, one of the most important parts of college is for students to socialize and explore their social as well as academic interests.

When searching for post-secondary programs, do not overlook community colleges both in your area and away. Many of these schools have excellent learning challenges support programs and generally they have significantly less costly tuition. They might also have smaller class sizes and classes maybe taught by professors versus teaching assistants. All these things are good for students with learning challenges. Most community colleges offer associate's degrees in a variety of fields which might be more attractive to some students with learning challenges than a four-year liberal arts curriculum. Some community colleges offer on-campus living and a college-like environment. Students can transfer from these programs to a four-year college or university whenever they choose to continue their education. Many courses at many community colleges will transfer to four-year colleges but be sure to double check on each school and course before you sign up.

When Asking for the College Application, Ask for Learning Challenges Program Information as Well

When initially contacting colleges or any post-secondary program for brochures and applications, it is important to ask them about their learning challenges support services. It is a good sign if the regular admissions staff is aware of the learning challenges support services. In addition, it is very valuable to contact the learning challenges support services separately to ask for their specific brochure. There are a number of schools which require one application for the college and a second application for the learning challenges support program. Often, the college acceptance is dependent on acceptance by the learning challenges support program. There might also be different application deadlines. Be sure you are clear on these requirements. It can get VERY confusing!

The Value of Visiting a School

After researching dozens of schools and narrowing the search to a handful, it is very important to visit the most promising programs. It is extremely important for a prospective student to have the regular admissions interview and to interview a member of the learning challenges support services staff, as well as to take a campus tour. Many programs with extensive learning challenges support programs require a personal interview with the student. Interviews can be scary. Role playing is helpful, but visiting a program or two during a high school student's freshman or sophomore year during a family vacation, or choosing a program near your home, will give your student a chance to experience a real interview and to practice interviewing skills. Choose a program that will not be one of the student's first choices so that there is less pressure and little downside to the interview. In this way, the student can become familiar with the process and more comfortable when the "real" interviews take place. Parents should remind their children how lucky the program will be to get them if they choose that program.

The Value of Staying Overnight at a School

Many programs allow prospective students to spend a night in the dorms. Overnights must be booked in advance when setting up the admissions appointments. If a program does not allow overnights, I would certainly question, why not? It is invaluable to stay overnight at a program if you can. By doing so, a prospective student can see the different social groups and judge how mature the other students in the program are. It is sort of like being behind the scenes in the evening when "the salespeople" are not present. When you are at the interview and on the campus tour, everyone emphasizes the positives of the campus and is on their best behavior. However, by spending the night, a student can often get a good gut feeling about the school. I eliminated one college because the girls in the dorm were so catty and cliquey with each other that I wanted no part of that school.

The College Essay

The college essay is a wonderful opportunity for a student with learning challenges to show what he or she has accomplished through the years. This is a moment in which a student can really shine. Many college applications will have specific topics on which to write, but most will also allow you to develop your own topic. This is a great opportunity to write about your learning challenges and how you have found ways to compensate for your weaknesses. Be sure and take advantage of this opportunity. My college essay won me a scholarship at Ohio Wesleyan University. You have a real story to tell too.

I am including here the essay that I submitted to colleges my junior year in high school as an example of the kind of compelling case a student with learning challenges can make to admissions departments at colleges and other programs. Your story will, of course, be a different one, but as long as you speak from your heart, I believe you will reach theirs.

My College Essay

(As submitted to colleges in 1995. It has purposely not been edited since.)

On the morning of December 22, 1983, anxious with thoughts of Christmas, I was an excited six-year-old pretending to be Black Beauty while trying to wait patiently for my mother to put on her make-up. After she finally finished dressing, we walked downstairs for our late-morning snack. As usual I requested vanilla ice cream, my favorite at that time. In the middle of eating, my head suddenly jerked back and fell forward into my ice cream, and then I toppled off the chair. I became nauseated, dizzy and disoriented. I did not know what had hit me, and nobody could have guessed that at that moment the direction of my life would change completely.

My mother immediately called 911 and the paramedics rushed me to the hospital. A CAT scan revealed in medical terms an aneurysm of the anterior artery of the posterior temporal lobe. The only option was for the surgeon to clip the bleeding artery. The operation lasted eight hours, leaving me unconscious for the next three days. When I awoke, I could understand everything people said, but when I tried to talk, only nonsense came out. I could not feel the right side of my body. I did not understand what had happened to me, but even in my confusion, I somehow knew that I could not look back, but that I had to go on from there.

I spent the next several years of my life working continuously to re-learn skills that I had lost and to develop new, compensatory strategies. After three weeks in the hospital, I finally returned home, but not to school. Instead, therapists came to my home every day. I spent endless hours learning how to walk again. I struggled for months to get around with a brace on my right leg, using a walker like I had seen elderly people use. After the physical therapist left, an occupational therapist came to exercise my right arm and hand. With the occupational therapist I spent my time practicing picking up objects, stretching my arms and learning to use my left hand instead of my right. My day was not complete until I finished working with a speech/language therapist, developing my expressive language skills. The physical therapy paid off first. Within a year or two, I could not only walk unaided, but run, swim and ride horseback almost as well as before.

Having to re-learn all of these basic skills sometimes embarrassed me because I saw my friends learning to ride their bicycles while I was just learning to walk again. When they visited and talked about swimming and playing, I was re-learning the names of fruits and vegetables. I did not get too upset about my situation, though, because I felt that if I worked hard enough, I would be able to "fix" everything.

Later that spring, I enrolled in a special school for the deaf. Soon I discovered that being the only hearing child in a school for the deaf was fun. The teachers tended to forget, and I overheard the most fascinating gossip. Over the next two and half years, those gifted teachers helped me to re-gain my speech completely. I appreciated their efforts because losing my speech presented the most frustrating obstacle for me and for others trying to communicate with me. I remember a time I spent almost thirty minutes just trying to get out the words to describe a squirrel climbing a tree. I often struggled vainly to express the ideas and feelings that filled my mind.

After what seemed like forever to me at that age, the drills I practiced for sounds and word pronunciations ended in success. I learned to talk again. In fact, I became so talkative; my therapist jokingly asked my parents if they really wanted me to continue my therapy or whether they might prefer me to remain mute.

My next challenge was to develop my reading skills. I attended for four years a local grade school dedicated to remediation for students with learning disabilities. I worked as hard on my reading as I had on my speech, but I did not achieve quite the same success. I still struggle somewhat with reading, so I find ways to compensate. I use books-on-tape and sometimes a reading scanner. I do not allow the barriers I face in reading to stop me from achieving my ambitions.

To further my educational goals, I enrolled in Brehm Preparatory School, a college preparatory boarding school specializing in education for students with learning disabilities. Even though I had to leave home at only thirteen, I approached this new challenge optimistically, an attitude that proved to be helpful to me. At Brehm, I learned to understand my learning disabilities and to compensate for them effectively. In my third year at Brehm I felt ready to try a regular high school. Most of the staff at Brehm did not think I was prepared to leave. They tried to discourage me from taking this next step, but I felt confident that I would succeed. One teacher supported my decision though, and helped me to keep up my hopes. Often in my life, when the experts have doubted my ability and potential, I learned to set my own standards and to rely on my own self-assessments and judgment when setting my goals.

From the first day I walked into Ladue High School, I have loved every moment of it. Being at a "normal" school was what I had been working toward for so many years. I felt I had finally arrived! It was different. My previous school had only fifty students and classes capped at eight. Ladue services over one thousand students, sometimes in classes of 25. Ladue's teachers have no training in special education so

I decided to start my sophomore year with a conservative course load. Going into my junior year, I selected courses more ambitiously. Against my counselor's advice, I enrolled in upper level English courses. I surprised him by achieving an A and an Honor's grade in those classes. I ended my junior year with straight A's, and I felt ready to move ahead to a new venture. Over the summer I successfully completed a statistics course at a local college, and this fall I enrolled in an Advanced Placement European history class. These academic successes mean a lot to me but I see them primarily as doors opening to the next level of achievement.

College will bring new challenges, but I know I have the tenacity to keep long-term goals in clear focus even when I face extended setbacks. College will be the next step closer to achieving my ultimate goal: to complete my doctorate in psychology and establish a private family and pediatric counseling practice.

Having an aneurysm has caused significant disadvantages. I have spent much of my childhood with therapists, tutors and boarding schools. I have been forced to re-define myself, to come to terms with who I am, and to determine what is truly important to me earlier than most people have to do. I have always needed to work longer hours than my friends and to contend with the inconvenience of arranging for books-on-tape and untimed testing

appointments. My standardized test scores do not reflect my
ability. Occasionally, I still run into people who doubt my
ability to succeed, and that is disheartening.

Coping with a learning difference throughout most of my
life has surprisingly brought me many advantages too. I have
learned not to fear hard work. I have learned the value of
time management and self discipline. I have learned to be
insightful and honest about my strengths and limitations and
to communicate them to others in a way that inspires them to
become committed to my success. I have learned to live away
from home at an early age. I know that life holds very little
that I cannot overcome. I have learned to believe in myself.
Always, I have found wonderful people, whose belief in me
has inspired me to take chances. I understand that life is
unpredictable, and I appreciate every moment of it. Most
importantly, I have learned that happiness is realizing that
what I have worked for so hard is what I truly want.

The Thank-You Letters

It is very important for a prospective student to write thank-you letters after every interview for both the admissions interview and the learning challenges program interview. It helps colleges to start a file on the student. It also portrays a student as mature and shows that the student has an interest in the school. A thank-you letter might not mean the difference between admission and rejection; however, if you and another applicant have the same qualifications, a thank-you letter might help to tilt the scales.

After Acceptance

Open communication with your post-secondary program's support services department and begin to arrange for whatever accommodations and support services you know you will need.

Register for courses as early as you can. Many colleges and programs allow early registration for their students with learning challenges. At my college, the earliest time possible for freshman course enrollment was May. After choosing courses, I immediately sent a letter to all of my new professors. The letter briefly introduced me as an incoming freshman with learning challenges and explained that I needed the syllabus for each course in order for me to obtain copies of the textbooks in a timely fashion so I could have them converted to audio by the beginning of fall semester.

Many programs will send a "generic" letter to professors about accommodations for students with learning challenges. However, these letters might be sent too late or be too "generic" to truly benefit the student. I recommend sending your own letter to each professor, similar to the letters I recommended in Strategy Eight that you used in high school. You can make your specific needs clear and stand out from your peers.

I spent a good deal of my pre-college summer putting ads in the college town paper and telephone-interviewing tutors who would be able to help me with my courses for the next four years. I am not against peer tutors, but I was not willing to risk my first semester of my freshman year on the chance of having a poor peer tutor instead of simply finding someone more mature and professional. In spite of face-to-face interviews before classes started, it took me several tries to find the right tutor. However, one of them stuck with me through my entire four years. He was a great guy with a lot of patience, and I will always be grateful for his time and help.

Course Load

Even though many advisors will tell you to take your mandatory courses first, I encourage students to take at least one course that they will love their first semester freshman year. This might be the most challenging semester in college, and I believe that if one doesn't take at least one class one loves, it is easy to become discouraged and burned out. I also recommend taking the lightest possible load the first semester.

Burnout

Burnout is a real hazard and something to guard against. It might hit at any time. Because students with learning and social challenges must work so much harder than their peers, they are very susceptible to burnout. Some students might need a break between senior year in high school and taking on the challenges of a post-secondary program. Many colleges and post-secondary programs will allow a student, once accepted, to "defer" attendance for a semester or a year. This is not an option to choose lightly, but it is an option.

For me, burnout hit after my college graduation. I knew I needed to go to graduate school, but I just couldn't face four more years of struggle without a break to recharge my batteries. Through my undergraduate years at school, I had fallen in love with the state of Maine, and I wanted to stay there for one more year before grad school. I loved the weather, and I adored the cold and beautiful white snow. After graduation I found a wonderful place in Maine to stay for the year. It was a beautiful property, built in 1770, with an interesting historical background. It looked out onto the Kennebec River. I was fortunate enough to find great neighbors who treated me as one of their grandkids, and who checked in on me weekly just to see if I was still alive. It was very neat to look out my window and see my horses grazing there. It was a very magical year and an opportunity to recharge my batteries. It seemed as if I had been working non-stop since I was six. Everyone should give himself or herself a break now and then.

Starting the Journey
A Timeline

Below is a checklist and time line that my mother and I found useful in our search for my best fit post-secondary program. You might need to modify it for your special situation, but it is a good general plan.

Starting the Journey

A Timeline

Beginning the search for programs/schools

Prior to junior year

- Plan volunteer, job, sport, music, extracurricular and summer activities that will enhance the student's résumé and increase his or her life experiences.

- Begin to consider and research what type of school— vocational programs, post-graduate programs, two-year college, four-year college—is most appropriate.

- What type of learning challenges support program is most appropriate? (Structured Programs, Coordinated Services, Services.) Obtain learning challenges support program descriptions and application guidelines. (The learning challenges program within a college might require a separate application with different deadlines—a dual application.)

- Ensure that testing/documentation which validates the student's disability has been administered within the last two to three years and will be valid throughout the application process.

- Decide whether SAT/ACT will be taken.

- Submit documentation and apply for appropriate accommodations for SAT/ACT or any college placement tests, for example, Advanced Placement tests.

Prior to Senior Year

- Prepare academic résumé to be updated as needed.
- Select a mix of "stretch,"[9] "likely"[10] and "safety"[11] programs to visit.
- Participate in role playing interviews.
- Set up traveling dates to visit potential learning challenges programs and college admissions offices. This often requires two interviews per school.
- Compose and send a thank-you letter after each interview.
- Confirm SAT/ACT scores are on file to send out to colleges.
- Acquire application(s) from programs and colleges.

---

[9] A program for which the student would have the lowest chance of admission.
[10] A program for which the student would have a good chance of admission.
[11] A program for which the student has the best chance of admission.

Senior year

- Obtain reference letters.

- Write the essay required for school acceptance or submit a fine arts portfolio if applicable.

- Make sure you know the application deadlines for both the college and LD support program if needed.

- Mail application at least five days before the deadline and make sure that it includes a request for ACT/SAT scores to be sent to that program.

- Wait.

- Acceptance(s) confirmed.

- As a team, you and your family choose which program/school will be the best match for you.

- Make a final decision and notify the program/school of your selection.

- Send money to secure placement in the program/school.

- Write a Self-Advocacy Letter to have available when your courses are selected.

- Pre-enroll in first-semester classes over the summer. Many schools allow this for students with learning challenges.

- Make arrangements for audio texts if needed.

- Prepare for change and transition and time to say goodbye.
- Move on—leaving high school!
- Celebrate!!!!

Conclusion

There are many steps in finding the perfect post-secondary program for a student. By starting the process early you can avoid the stress caused by waiting until the last minute. This should be a fun process for parents and child. Students with learning challenges have worked exceptionally hard to achieve their present academic success and social maturity. This search is their reward for that hard work. There are many fine programs from which to choose. Keep in mind that students are choosing the program that is right for them—it is not the program choosing the student.

Appendix

Sample Letters, Information Lists & Questionnaires

For your convenience, all sample letters, information lists and questionnaires are available for you to download and personalize from my website: www.ilsinc.org.

Your name

Your address and phone number

Date

RE: AUDIO BOOKS

COURSE: (department and course number)

Dear Dr. X,

I am planning to take the above course with you this fall. I rely heavily on audio books because of my learning disability. I must order audio texts several months in advance to allow taping time if the book is not in stock.

I would be very grateful if you would send me a complete list of textbooks that you plan to use for the above course.

I would also be grateful for copies of any additional printed materials, including handouts that you plan to assign so I can arrange to have them taped.

If you are using only portions of any book, please note exactly which chapters or pages will be assigned. Because time is so short between semesters, my readers can record only the necessary portions.

Audio transcriptions require:

FOR BOOKS:

Title

Author

Publisher

Edition (critical)

Copyright Date

ISBN number

FOR OTHER PRINTED MATERIAL: a legible copy. I can pick up the list from your office, you can put it in the mail (your address) or you can e-mail it to me at (your e-mail address), whichever is most convenient for you. If you have any questions, I can be reached at (your phone number).

I sincerely appreciate this extra effort on your part and I look forward to being in your course this winter.

Sincerely,

(Your Name)

Your name

Your address and phone number

Date

Course: (department and course number)

I would like to take a few moments to tell you a little about myself and to explain why I need the accommodations I am requesting in your course. (See attached IEP.)

(Here, talk about your history/accomplishments.) For example: In third grade I was diagnosed with a cluster of learning disabilities that impact my ability to read and process the written word. I attended XYZ Preparatory School in XYZ, until this year. XYZ is a prep school dedicated to empowering students with learning disabilities. I have worked hard to understand my learning disabilities and to develop specific strategies to compensate for them. I am looking forward to my first year at ABC High School as the next step in my academic career. I love learning and exposure to new ideas. I am organized, motivated, hard-working, and am totally serious about my studies. My hope is to attend DEF College, which my father attended. My dream is to become a teacher of history. (Or state whatever positive characteristics and hopes and dreams you believe you have.)

Unfortunately, I still need a number of accommodations to help me learn and to help you measure accurately what I have actually learned. The aids I use out of class are: subject area tutoring, audio books, a computer reading scanner for typed materials not available on tape, a reader for poor-quality printed material that won't scan, and a computer voice recognition dictation program. I rely heavily on "spell check" and word processing for as much of my work as I can. When I am pressed for time, I dictate to a scribe.

Accommodations I am requesting in your course are:

AUDIO BOOKS
Accurate and timely syllabi for texts, all handouts and outside reading assignments.

The MOST critical accommodation for me is acquiring a complete syllabus two to three months before a course so I have adequate time to order any material that is not currently available on audio. I rely heavily on audio of all printed material. These processes can take several month's lead time. My backup is a scanner; however the scanning process is time-consuming and if handouts are of poor quality, my scanner can't process them at all and I must arrange for someone to read them to me.

EXAMS AND QUIZZES

Extended time for tests

Quiet testing area

Tests taped or read to me by a proctor

I can read, but it is still such a difficult process that I can lose the exact meaning of a question. By reading along with the proctor (or a tape), I can be sure of clearly understanding what your test questions are asking. The reason for requesting extended time is that working with a reader, tape or scribe simply takes longer.

PEER NOTE-TAKERS

In some classes, the process of writing and spelling is so difficult and time-consuming that I cannot observe what the teacher is demonstrating on the board. Peer notes free me up to concentrate fully on what the teacher is presenting. I usually transcribe peer notes outside of class.

SCRIBING

Some exams and quizzes

Some written assignments

If I dictate, I can often be more creative and organize my thoughts better and save a great deal of time.

READING ALOUD

I prefer not to be asked to read aloud in class because I still stumble over many words. I like to actively participate in class in other ways.

(List whatever accommodations you need to succeed and explain why you need them and how they help you learn.)

My reading rate is improving and I am working hard to reduce my need for these accommodations. I appreciate your willingness to help me work around my learning disability and I understand that it takes extra effort on your part as well as on mine.

Thank you for taking the time to read this. I hope it will help you to understand a bit better how and why I use some of the accommodations I am requesting and that it will help you help me to achieve my goals in your course this year. If there is anything I can explain further, please ask me at any time.

Sincerely,

(Your Name)

Sample Evaluation Letter to Teachers
Parent Name
Parent Address
Parent Telephone Number

Date

Name of Teacher

Teacher's Address

Or High School Address

Dear Mr./Mrs. (Name of Teacher),

I know how much (Name of Student) appreciated your instruction, support and encouragement throughout this past (quarter, semester, year), as well as your understanding of his/her learning disability. He/She enjoyed your course immensely. As his/her parent I want to SINCERELY thank you and also to ask one further favor.

This was (Name of Student's) first year at (Name of High School) and her first year at a school not specifically devoted to students with learning disabilities. Thanks in great part to teachers like you, it has been a successful transition and we are very pleased and proud of the work (Name of Student) has accomplished.

He/She strongly desires to attend college and at this point is interested in a degree in (Degree Interest). Fortunately, there are a number of colleges with comprehensive LD support programs and I am trying to gain practical knowledge of his/her specific academic strengths and weaknesses in order to prepare him/her for college demands and to match him/her up with the program that will give him/her the greatest opportunity for success.

I would be very grateful if you would take a few minutes of your time to share your candid assessment of him/her as a student over the past quarter/semester and to give me any of your insights that would help us in planning his/her academic future.

1) I think it would be particularly helpful for us to understand:

His/her general strengths as a student?

_____

_____

_____

Your suggestions of what he/she or his/her parents could do to build on them?

_____

_____

_____

His/her specific weaknesses as a student?

_____

_____

_____

Any specific steps you feel he/she or his/her parents could do over the next year and a half to compensate for weaknesses or remediate them?

_____

_____

_____

2) Please touch on some of the following that strike you as particularly important:

His/her attitude, motivation?

_____

_____

_____

His/her ability to seek help needed appropriately?

_____

_____

_____

His/her ability to work independently?

_____

_____

_____

His/her ability to cope with criticism, setbacks, etc.?

_____

_____

_____

His/her organizational skills?

_____

_____

_____

How he/she coped with the normal workload?

_____

_____

_____

How much and what kind of extra support he/she
required of you in class?

_____

_____

_____

How much and what kind of extra support he/she
required of you outside of class?

_____

_____

_____

How he/she handled class participation?

_____

_____

_____

How he/she handled the homework load?

_____

_____

_____

Information that you did not have about (Name of Student) that would have been useful for you to have before teaching (Name of Student) or think would be useful to future teachers?

_____

_____

_____

Would you be comfortable writing a college letter of recommendation for (Name of Student) in the future?

_____

_____

_____

I know this is a lot to ask of you in the middle of a busy school year (or during your busy summer), but it would be enormously valuable to us for planning (Name for Student's) future.

Sincerely,

(Name of Parent)

Note: Include a self-addressed stamped envelope and write a thank you note to any teacher who takes the time to send you a response—even if you are not thrilled with the content.

Audio Books /CD/Download Sources

Learning Ally (formally called Recordings for the Blind and Dyslexic), Princeton, NJ 1-800-221-4792.

Learning Ally has the largest library of audio textbooks for all ages. Not-for-profit.

www.learningally.org

BookShare

www.bookshare.org

Similar to Learning Ally, but not free.

Books-on-Tape, Newport Beach, CA 1-800-252-6996.

For-profit, this is a large library of classic fiction and nonfiction available for a rental fee.

www.booksontape.com

Blackstone Audio books, Ashland, OR 1-800-729-2665.

For-profit, this is a large library of classic fiction and nonfiction available for a rental fee.

www.blackstoneaudio.com

Wolfner Library for the Blind and Physically Handicapped, Jefferson City, MO tape library, is free to handicapped residents of Missouri.

www.sos.mo.gov/wolfner/

Note: Most states have a service similar to Wolfner. Contact your local library.

LIST OF ADAPTIVE TECHNOLOGY SOURCES

Franklin Spellers

www.franklin.com

Scanners and OCR Programs

OpenBook (LD friendly)

www.freedomscientific.com

SARA (all in one kit)

www.freedomscientific.com

Kurzweil 1000TM (Blind/Low Vision Group)

www.kurzweiledu.com

Hand Scanners

The Quicktionary Reading Pen

Reading Pens and Dictionaries

www.quick-pen.com

www.innovationhouse.com

Speech Recognition Software

Dragon Naturally Speaking

www.nuance.com

Screen Readers

NaturalReader

A good free software.

www.naturalreaders.com

TextAloud

For Windows PC that converts your text from MS Word Documents, Web Pages, Emails and PDF Files into natural-sounding speech.

www.nextup.com

Read Please

A good free software.

www.readplease.com

EReader (Cast)

www.cast.org

JAWS (Freedom Scientific) (Blind/Low Vision Group)

www.freedomscientific.com

Kurzweil 3000

www.kurzweiledu.com

Word Anticipation Programs

Co-Writer

www.donjohnston.com

SoothSayer Word Prediction

www.ahf-net.com

Interview Questions for
School/College/University Staff

Program: _____

Date Completed: _____

General Questions about the Learning Disability Support Program or to be modified for your applicable learning, social or physical challenge.

Is there a LD Program?	Yes/No
Is there a specific person in charge of the LD program?	Yes/No
If so, what are his/her qualifications?	
How long has the program been in existence?	
Is there a central place where students can go to access help?	Yes/No
Is diagnostic testing required for admission to program?	Yes/No
If so, is it done by program personnel?	Yes/No

What is the cost?	$
Is the ACT required?	Yes/No
What is the minimum score for admission?	
Is the SAT required?	Yes/No
What is the minimum score for admission?	
Are there other admissions requirements for the LD program?	Yes/No
If so, what are they?	
Are waivers granted for classes which are impacted by the learning disability? (Example: Foreign language waiver?)	Yes/No
Is there a new student orientation for the LD program?	Yes/No
Is there any kind of priority registration or assistance in class registration for students in the LD program?	Yes/No
Are remedial/developmental courses required?	Yes/No
Are any other college preparatory classes offered?	Yes/No
Is a foreign language required?	Yes/No

Is there a foreign language waiver?	Yes/No
Is there a flow chart that indicates which staff is responsible for which services?	Yes/No

Tutors:

Are tutors provided?	Yes/No
Are tutors assigned by subject area?	Yes/No
Are the procedures for requesting/obtaining tutors clearly defined?	Yes/No
Is there an extra cost for tutors?	Yes/No
Is so, what is it?	$
Is there a tutor supervisor?	Yes/No
What kind of training do tutors receive?	
Professional or peer tutors?	
Who makes the arrangements for meeting with tutor(s)?	
Where do you meet with your tutor(s)?	

Course Accommodations:

Un-timed tests	Yes/No
Note-takers	Yes/No
Extended time	Yes/No

Computers	Yes/No
Readers: for assignments	Yes/No
Use of tape recorders in lecture	Yes/No
Copies of class notes	Yes/No
Audio Books /CD	Yes/No
Proof readers	Yes/No
Calculators for tests	Yes/No

Library:

Assistance or training for use of library?	Yes/No

Computers:

Is there a computer lab?	Yes/No
Is help available?	Yes/No
How many computers are available?	#
Are printers available?	Yes/No
Are scanners available?	Yes/No
Other computer equipment?	
Are laptop computers allowed in classes for note-taking?	Yes/No

Student Advocacy:

Is there a person to act as a mediator between student and faculty?	Yes/No
How often do advisors meet with students?	
Are there written procedures for advocating?	Yes/No
Is there opportunity for students to self-advocate?	Yes/No

Counseling Services:

Career Planning?	Yes/No
Job coaching/training?	Yes/No
Individual counseling?	Yes/No
LD support group?	Yes/No
Problem solving assistance?	Yes/No
Transition planning?	Yes/No

General Program Questions:

What is the average student/teacher ratio in the classroom?	
What percentage of graduates have jobs waiting when they graduate?	%

What percentage of graduates have learning disabilities?	%

Transportation:

Is there a shuttle service?	Yes/No
Is there public transportation?	Yes/No
If so, is it on campus?	Yes/No

Money:

Do students manage their own money?	Yes/No
(Brehm Preparatory School, 2005)	
Does this program have additional LD support beyond what is required by law?	Yes/No
Is there an additional cost over tuition for the LD support program?	Yes/No
If so, what is the cost?	$
How many students are currently being served by the program?	#
Is there a maximum number of hours per week of services a student can use?	Yes/No
What is the ratio of LD support staff to students with LD?	

How many full-time staff members work in the support program?	
Part time?	
Are there LD specialists available?	Yes/No
Are students allowed to take fewer classes and still maintain their full-time status?	Yes/No
Are tutors professional tutors or peer tutors?	Professional/Peer
Will teachers restructure their tests to accommodate the needs of students with LD?	Yes/No
Is there a computer reading machine available?	Yes/No
Is computer dictation software available?	Yes/No
What do you perceive as the weaknesses of the program? What are your overall feelings about the program?	
(Phelps, 2000)	

Are there any concerns for the support program's future?	Yes/No
Has the support program been evaluated in the past?	Yes/No
By whom?	
Is the evaluation summary available for students/families?	Yes/No
(ERIC Clearinghouse, 1989)	

Interview Questions for Students

Program: _____

Date Completed: _____

General Questions about the Learning Disability Support Program or to be modified for your applicable learning, social or physical challenge.

Is there an LD Program?	Yes/No
Is there a specific person in charge of the LD program?	Yes/No
Is there a central place where students can go to access help?	Yes/No
Is diagnostic testing required for admission to the program?	Yes/No
If so, is it done by program personnel?	Yes/No
What other admissions requirements did you have to meet?	
Are waivers granted for classes which are affected by the learning disability?	Yes/No

Was there a new student orientation for the LD program?	Yes/No
Is there any kind of priority registration or assistance in registration for students in the LD program?	Yes/No
Are remedial/developmental courses required?	Yes/No
Are any other college preparatory classes offered?	Yes/No
Is a foreign language required?	Yes/No
Is there a flow chart that indicates which staff is responsible for which services?	Yes/No

Tutors:

Are tutors provided?	Yes/No
Are tutors assigned by subject area?	Yes/No
Are the procedures for requesting/obtaining tutors clearly defined?	Yes/No
Who makes the arrangements for meeting with tutor(s)?	
Where does a student meet with a tutor(s)?	

Course Accommodations:

Un-timed tests	Yes/No
Note-takers	Yes/No
Extended time for assignments/tests by request	Yes/No
Computers	Yes/No
Readers: for assignments	Yes/No
Use of tape recorders in lecture	Yes/No
Copies of class notes	Yes/No
Audio Books /CD	Yes/No
Proofreaders	Yes/No
Calculators for tests	Yes/No

Library:

Assistance or training for use of library?	Yes/No

Computers:

Is there a computer lab?	Yes/No
Is help available?	Yes/No
How many computers are available?	#
What kind of computers?	
Are printers available?	Yes/No
Are scanners available?	Yes/No

Other computer equipment?	
What assistive technology is available?	

Student Advocacy:

Is there a person to act as a mediator between student and faculty?	Yes/No
How often do advisors meet with students?	
Are there written procedures for advocating?	Yes/No
Is there opportunity for students to self-advocate?	Yes/No

Counseling Services:

Career Planning?	Yes/No
Job coaching/training?	Yes/No
Individual counseling?	Yes/No
Learning Disability support group?	Yes/No
Problem solving assistance?	Yes/No
Transition planning?	Yes/No

Transportation:	
Is there a shuttle service?	Yes/No
Is there public transportation?	Yes/No
If so, is it on campus or near?	Yes/No
Money:	
Do students manage their own money?	Yes/No
(Brehm Preparatory School, 2005)	
Is there a maximum number of hours per week of support services a student can use?	Yes/No
What is the ratio of LD support staff to students with LD?	
How many full-time staff members work in the support program?	
Part time?	
Are there LD specialists available?	Yes/No
Are students allowed to take fewer classes and still maintain their full-time status?	Yes/No
Are tutors professional tutors or peer tutors? Both?	Professional/ Peer/Both
Will teachers restructure their tests to accommodate the needs of students with LD?	Yes/No

Is there a computer reading machine available?	Yes/No
Is computer dictation software available?	Yes/No
What do you perceive as the strengths of the Learning Disability program?	
What do you perceive as the weaknesses /challenges of the program?	
What are your overall feelings about the program?	
Do you feel that there are enough staff members to accommodate your needs?	Yes/No
Do you feel welcome when you go to discuss or request services?	Yes/No
Does the staff know who you are when you go in?	Yes/No
Is the staff friendly?	Yes/No

Is it simple to request accommodations?	Yes/No
Describe the process you must go through to request accommodations:	
Have you spoken with an LD specialist through the program?	Yes/No
Is it easy to get a tutor?	Yes/No
Is it easy to find/obtain a new tutor if you feel you do not work well with your current tutor?	Yes/No
What do you think the attitude of faculty is toward cooperating with your accommodations?	
What are your class sizes?	
Are you aware of any discrimination from other students because of your LD?	Yes/No
If yes, please comment:	
(Phelps, 2000)	

Starting the Journey
A Timeline

Beginning the search for programs/schools

Prior to junior year

- Plan volunteer, job, sport, music, extracurricular and summer activities that will enhance the student's résumé and increase his or her life experiences.

- Begin to consider and research what type of school, vocational programs, post-graduate ("pg") program, two-year college, or four-year college is most appropriate.

- What type of learning challenges support program is most appropriate? (Structured Programs, Coordinated Services, Services). Obtain learning challenges support program descriptions and application guidelines. (The learning challenges program within a college might require a separate application with different deadlines—a dual application.)

- Ensure that testing/documentation which validates the student's disability has been administered within the last two or three years and will be valid throughout the application process.

- Decide if SAT/ACT will be taken.
- Submit documentation and apply for appropriate accommodations for SAT/ACT or any college placement tests, for example, Advanced Placement tests.

Prior to Senior year

- Prepare academic résumé to be updated as needed.
- Select a mix of "stretch," "likely" and "safety" programs to visit.
- Participate in role playing interviews.
- Set up traveling dates to visit potential learning challenges programs and college admissions offices. This often requires two interviews per school.
- Compose and send a thank-you letter after each interview.
- Confirm that SAT/ACT scores are on file to send out to colleges.
- Acquire application(s) from programs and colleges.

Senior year

- Obtain reference letters.
- Write the essay required for school acceptance, or submit a fine arts portfolio if applicable.
- Make sure you know the application deadlines for both the college and LD support program if needed.

- Mail application at least five days before the deadline and make sure that it includes a request for ACT/SAT scores to be sent to that program.

- Wait.

- Acceptance(s) confirmed

- As a team, you and your family choose which program/school will be the best match for you.

- Make a final decision and notify program/school of your selection.

- Send money to secure placement in program/school.

- Write a Self-advocacy Letter to have available when your courses are selected.

- Pre-enroll in first-semester courses over the summer. Many schools allow this for students with learning challenges.

- Make arrangements for audio texts if needed.

- Prepare for change and transition and time to say goodbye

- Move on—Leaving high school!

- Celebrate!!!!

References

(2013). American Psychiatric Association. *Diagnostic and statistical manual of mental disorders: DSM-5*. Washington, D.C: American Psychiatric Association.

(2000). American Psychiatric Association, *Diagnostic and Statistical Manual of Mental Disorders* (4th ed., text revision). Washington, D.C.: American Psychiatric Publications.

(2005). Transition packet [brochure]. Carbondale, IL: Brehm Preparatory School.

(2007). *Colleges for Students with Learning Disabilities or AD/HD*. (8th ed.). Lawrenceville, NJ: Nelnet Company.

ERIC Clearinghouse on Handicapped and Gifted Children. (1989). *College Planning for Students with Learning Disability*. Reston, VA: ERIC Clearinghouse.

Kravets, M., & Wax, E. (2010). *K&W Guide to Colleges for Students with Learning Disabilities*. (10th ed.). New York: Random House.

(2011). *Peterson's Two-Year Colleges* (42nd ed.). Lawrenceville, NY: Nelnet Company.

Phelps, N. B. (2006, March). *Transition planning from high school to post-secondary or vocational training for the student with learning disabilities.* Paper presented at Learning Disability Association of America International Conference, Jacksonville, FL.

Phelps, N. B. (2000, February). *Adaptive technology and accommodations.* Paper presented at the Learning Disability Association of America International Conference, Reno, NV.

Phelps, N. B., & Collins, R. (1999, February). *Attitude, advocacy and adaptive technology: An LD student's strategies for success.* Paper presented at the Learning Disability Association of America International Conference, Atlanta, GA.

Thomson/Peterson's. (2003). Retrieved March 13, 2003, from http://www.petersons.com

(1954). W. A. Neilson et al. (Eds.), *Webster's new international dictionary of the English language, Second Edition Unabridged.* Springfield, MA: G.C. Merriam Co.

CHADD
http://www.ldanatl.org/aboutld/resources/frames.asp?top.asp+http://www.chadd.org/ July 30, 2008 Understanding AD/HD

Made in the USA
Charleston, SC
06 November 2015